GOOGLE WORKSPACE GUIDE:

CW00735335

Learn to Use Effortlessly and with Minimal Effort Through Explanations and Step-by-Step Screenshots

Copyright © 2023

Kevin Pitch

TABLE OF CONTENTS

1   INTRODUCTION

Google is a well-known technological corporation primarily recognized for its search engine, the most popular worldwide. Google's search engine is driven by a sophisticated algorithm that analyzes website content and assesses its relevance to a user's query. This enables Google to deliver the most relevant results even when consumers search for specialized or difficult issues.

Google's search engine quickly gained global popularity. 2000, it accounted for only 1% of the worldwide search market. By 2004, it had captured over 50% of the market, and today it has over 90%. Google's search engine has made it easier for people to find information online and has also contributed to the growth of the internet economy. Google's search engine has also significantly contributed to enhancing internet accessibility. In the early days of the Internet, it was challenging to find information. There were many different websites, and knowing which ones were reliable or up to date took a lot of work. Google's search engine made it easier to find information by organizing it and ranking it according to its relevance. This made it possible for people to find the needed information, even if they did not know where to start. Google's search engine has also made the Internet more accessible to people with disabilities. The search engine can be used with screen readers and other assistive technologies, making it possible for people with visual impairments to use the Internet. Google has also developed features that make it easier for people with disabilities to use its products, such as large fonts and high-contrast text. Google started as a search engine but quickly expanded into other areas like email, productivity apps, and cloud computing. Gmail, a free email service with a large storage capacity and various features, was one of Google's first services after its search engine. Gmail quickly gained popularity and is now one of the most popular email services in the world. Google has also ventured into other areas, such as maps, productivity apps, and cloud computing. Google Maps is a handy mapping tool that allows users to find directions, view satellite imagery, and get real-time traffic information. Google also has a slew of productivity apps, like Google Docs, which enables users to create and edit documents; Google Spreadsheets, which makes spreadsheets; and Google Slides, which develops customizable presentations. Businesses can easily build and deploy applications, manage data, and use the Google Cloud Platform.

1.1   What's Google Workspace?

Google Workspace is a cloud-based suite with various productivity tools for individuals and businesses. These tools include Gmail, Docs, Sheets, Slides, Drive, Calendar, and Meet. Google Workspace allows users to create, edit, and share documents, spreadsheets, presentations, and more online. It also provides a secure place to store and access files from anywhere. For businesses of all sizes, the popularity of using Google Workspace has skyrocketed because it is easy to use, secure, and scalable. Google also offers a variety of pricing plans to fit the needs of different businesses. Here are some of the benefits of using Google Workspace:

- Increased productivity: Google Workspace tools can help you be more productive by allowing you to work on documents, spreadsheets, and presentations online. You can engage and work together with people online.
- Enhanced security: Google is known for its protection and is trusted by many individuals and businesses worldwide. Google uses various security measures to protect your data, including encryption, two-factor authentication, and malware scanning.
- Improved scalability: Google Workspace can be scaled to meet the needs of your business. Especially when a company or firm has grown, you can readily and easily add more users and even increase the storage capacity of your Google Workspace account.

Google Workspace is a great option if you are looking for a cloud-based productivity suite to help you be more productive and secure. In October 2020, Google changed the name of G Suite to Google Workspace to better reflect the suite's focus on helping people work together more effectively.

Here are some of the reasons why Google changed the name of G Suite:

- To better reflect the suite's focus on collaboration, Google Workspace includes various tools that help people collaborate more effectively, such as Google Docs, Google Sheets, and Google Slides.
- To emphasize the fact that Google Workspace is a cloud-based platform, Google Workspace is a cloud-based platform that can be accessed from anywhere, which makes it ideal for businesses and individuals who need to work remotely.
- To simplify the name: The previous name, G Suite, was confusing because it could be interpreted as referring to a suite of applications for businesses (G Suite for Business) or applications for education (G Suite for Education). The new name, Google Workspace, is more straightforward to understand.

Google Workspace is a tool that can help empower businesses and individuals to be more productive and collaborative. The new name reflects the suite's focus on these areas and makes it easier for people to understand what Google Workspace is and what it can do. Speaking of tools, let us now dive into the different tools that Google Workspace offers. The following tools are accessible online through a web browser, from a Personal computer, a laptop, or a mobile device. The following tools included are the following:

- Gmail: Email service that allows you to send and receive emails, create, and manage labels, and filters.
- Google Docs: Word processing app that individuals can use to create, edit, and customize documents.
- Google Sheets: Spreadsheet app that allows you to create and edit spreadsheets and use formulas and functions.
- Google Slides: Presentation app that allows you to create and edit presentations and add animations and transitions.
- Google Drive: Storage service enabling users to store files via online cloud-based storage, which can be accessed anywhere and shared with others.
- Google Calendar: A Calendar app that helps track your appointments and events and receive reminders.
- Google Meet: Video conferencing service that individuals use to connect with others face-to-face or via audio, allows screen sharing and can record the meeting.
- Google Chat: Messaging app for chatting with others one-on-one or in groups, also allows file sharing and video chats.
- Google Sites: Website builder for creating and managing websites without coding knowledge.
- Google Keep: Note-taking app that creates and organizes notes, lists, and reminders.
- Google Forms: Form-building app that allows you to create and collect data from others.
- Google Jamboard: Collaborative whiteboard app that makes it easier to brainstorm and collaborate with others in real-time.

1.2   Target Audience and Business Application, Pricing and Plans.

Google Workspace caters to the needs of all businesses, whether it be a small shop, a new company, or a large enterprise. Google Workspace has services that make running a business easier and safer. But it is also aimed towards individuals needing cloud-based productivity tools for personal or work-related use. When we go strictly to the business side of Google Workspace. We can see that it has many applications which are crucial in growing a business. Although this can still apply to individuals.

Collaboration: Employees work together on documents, spreadsheets, presentations, and other files. Members can share files, track changes, and comment on documents in real time. This helps teams stay organized and productive and ensures everyone is on the same page.

Communication: Google Workspace has various tools like Gmail, Google Chat, and Google Meet. It makes it easier to get in touch and remain in contact with personnel through emails, chat, or even video conferences.

Storage: Google Workspace offers comprehensive storage space for your files. Most users can store their documents, spreadsheets, presentations, media, audio, and other files. These files are all stored and can be accessed anywhere on any device via Google Drive.

Security: Google Workspace has designed its security by using high levels of encryption both in transit and at rest, and Google offers a variety of security features to help protect your data.

With such powerful tools for both business and individual use, the question of whether the services of Google Workspace are free arises. The simple answer is that Google Workspace is a paid service, although a few free versions are available for download but with access to limited features and storage space. For example, Google Workspace Individual is a free plan for personal use, and Google Workspace for Nonprofits is a free plan for eligible organizations. Let us look at the pricing and plans available for Google Workspace. For accuracy purposes, all the information taken was from the official Google Workspace pricing page at https://workspace.google.com/pricing, and if pricing does change, refer to the link provided.

Plan	Price	Features
Basic	$6 per user per month	Gmail, Google Drive, Google Docs, Google Sheets, Google Slides, Google Calendar, Google Meet, and Google Chat
Business Starter	$12 per user per month	All features of Basic, plus Google Forms, Google Sites, and Google Keep
Business Standard	$18 per user per month	All features of Business Starter, plus Google Voice, Google Vault, and Google Cloud Search
Business Plus	$21 per user per month	All features of Business Standard, plus Google Advanced Protection Program, and more storage space
Enterprise Essentials	$25 per user per month	All features of Business Plus, plus additional security features
Enterprise Standard	$30 per user per month	All features of Enterprise Essentials, plus additional features for large enterprises
Enterprise Plus	$35 per user per month	All features of Enterprise Standard, plus additional features for very large enterprises

Each plan offers a lot, and the more you pay, the more features become available for you with larger storage space. However, individuals and small businesses may not need such robust features, and even just getting the Basic or Business Starter plans may already be enough. Still, of course, this all depends on the needs of the business.

1.3 How To Use This Guide

It is getting harder for people to get accustomed to using Google Workspace apps without prior knowledge or being tech savants. With Google Workspace offering so many services for users, utilizing all applications could seem confusing. No worries, this book is a comprehensive guide to Google's different applications and services. It covers assorted topics, from productivity apps like Gmail and Docs to cloud storage services like Google Drive, Google Cloud Platform, and more. The book also provides detailed instructions, screenshots, or images on navigating and properly utilizing each service.

2   GETTING STARTED

2.1   Setting up your Google Workspace Account

Now that we have a basic understanding of Google Workspace, let us now make an account. The following steps will guide you through the setup.

1. Go to the Google Workspace website: https://workspace.google.com/. The site should look something like the image below.

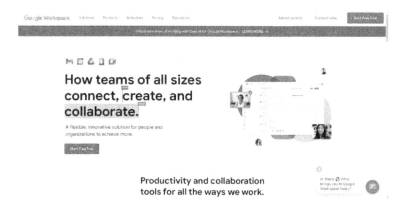

2. From the main webpage click Start free trial.

3. Fill out the information on the next page. This includes the Business name, selecting the number of employees, and the country. Then click next.

4.   Fill out your contact information and email address. Then click Next.

5.   If your business has a domain, then click the "Yes, I have one I can use" and if you do not have one yet, select "No, I need one."

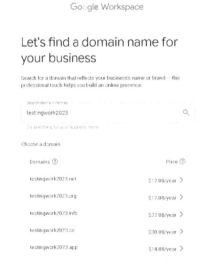

This next section will guide you on what to do when you do not own a domain and select: No, I need one." For those who already have a domain, you can go to section No. 9 of this guide.

6.   Input a domain name and click the spyglass button to find an appropriate domain. Google will automatically give you several options and provide different yearly subscriptions. This is a separate payment from a Google Workspace subscription. There are other domain providers, but most have subscription fees, and their prices may vary from what Google offers. If you stick with Google, select a domain name from the appropriate list to continue.

7.	The next page will show you a summary of the domain you created and what the domain is for; please review this page and then click the Next button.

8.	Fill in your business information and click Next, and you should now have successfully made a domain. Afterward, you will go to the "Create a username and password for your account" section No.11 of this guide.

9.	Enter your domain name and click Next.

10.   Review the domain information and click Next.

11.   Create a username and password for your account.

12.   Once you have completed creating your Google Workspace account, you must set up your business account and domain. Click on "Continue to Setup."

Your Google Workspace account has been created

Ready to set up your business account and get jj@jjtheloc.com working with Gmail? We'll walk you through each step.

CONTINUE TO SETUP

13.   Click "Activate" to set up the Gmail account for the business account.

After clicking activate, you will be taken to another page. You are required to sign into your domain provider. Click on "Sign in to activate" to continue. If the "Sign in to activate" is unavailable, you may do so manually by visiting your domain host.

If it is required for you to setup MX and DNS, go to section No.14 of this guide.
It may take a long time for your setup to complete. Depending on the domain provider and Google, you may have to wait for 5 to 10 minutes. Once it is done, you have completed the setup.

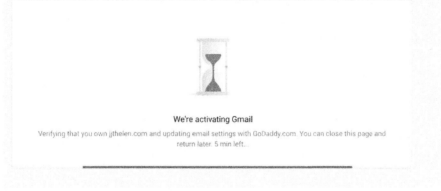

14.   Set up your email by adding MX records to your DNS records. Follow the on-screen instructions provided by Google.

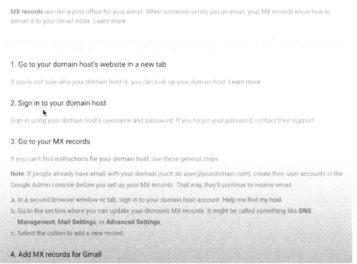

After logging in to your domain host. Look for the DNS Settings. A Sample picture is provided but will differ depending on your domain provider.

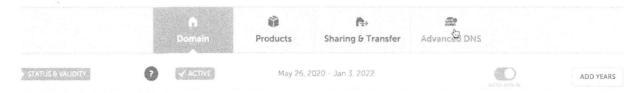

Locate Mail Settings and if it has no "Email Service" change it to "Custom MX."

Head back to the instructions page and follow the instructions on "Add MX Records for Gmail." You may want to copy the ASPMX.L.GOOGLE.COM; we will use this later.

3. Go to your MX records

If you can't find instructions for your domain host, use these general steps.

Note: If people already have email with your domain (such as *user@yourdomain.com*), create their user accounts in the Google Admin console *before* you set up your MX records. That way, they'll continue to receive email.

a. In a second browser window or tab, sign in to your domain host account. Help me find my host.

b. Go to the section where you can update your domain's MX records. It might be called something like **DNS Management**, **Mail Settings**, or **Advanced Settings**.

c. Select the option to add a new record.

4. Add MX records for Gmail

a. From the **Type** drop-down list, select **MX**.

b. In the **Name/Host/Alias** field, enter @ or leave it blank.

c. In the **Server/Mail Server/Value/Answer/Destination** field, enter **ASPMX.L.GOOGLE.COM.**.

d. In the **Priority** field, enter **1**.

e. In the **Time to Live (TTL)** field, enter **3600** or leave the default value.

f. Click **Save**.

Head back again to your domain host. On the MX Record, by following the instructions on the instruction page of Google, you will fill up the form, and it should look like the image below. Remember to save the changes after you have finished.

You will have to add four other MX records. Just follow the instructions and input them into the domain host.

g. Follow these same steps to add the MX records shown in this table. Start from the top of the table and enter as many as you have room for.

MX SERVER ADDRESS	PRIORITY
ALT1.ASPMX.L.GOOGLE.COM.	5
ALT2.ASPMX.L.GOOGLE.COM.	5
ALT3.ASPMX.L.GOOGLE.COM.	10
ALT4.ASPMX.L.GOOGLE.COM.	10

Add new records in the domain host by clicking the "Add New Record" button. An example is provided in the image below.

Type	Host	Value		TTL
MX Record	@	ASPMX.L.GOOGLE.COM.	1	Automatic

ADD NEW RECORD

Head back again to the Google instruction page, we now need to get the verification code by clicking the "Copy" button.

5. Get your verification code

COPY

Go back to your domain host. We will need to create another record, but this time, we will include the copied verification code and follow the instructions.

6. Add MX verification record

Add another MX record just like you did above. Only this time:

- In the **Server/Mail Server/Value/Answer/Destination** field, paste the **MX verification record** (ends in mx-verification.google.com) you copied above.

- In the **Priority** field, enter **15**.

MX Record	@	ALT2.ASPMX.L.GOOGLE.COM.	5	Automatic	🗑
MX Record	@	ALT3.ASPMX.L.GOOGLE.COM	10	Automatic	🗑
MX Record	@	ALT4.ASPMX.L.GOOGLE.COM	10	Automatic	🗑
MX Record	@	inrusciuua.mx-verification.google.com.	15	Automatic ▾	✓ ✗

Do not forget to save the changes.

Finally, head back again to the Google instruction page and click on "Activate Gmail," located at the bottom. A new page will pop up and start setting up Gmail with your domain host. If an error occurs, please check that all the values are correct, and if all the values input are right, retry the activation by clicking on the "Retry Activation" button.

If you still receive an error message even though all values are correct, you may have to wait a couple of hours before you can try to activate. Hopefully, that is not the case, but some individuals have reported this to happen, so be aware that you may have to wait a bit.

A successful activation will lead you to a new page, and it will say that your domain is verified, and your Gmail is activated.

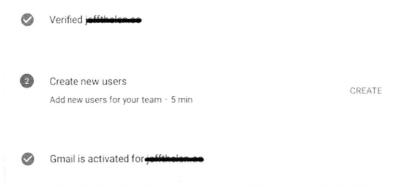

Congratulations on making it this far. You have successfully set up the MX records to your DNS records. You can also check your Gmail by going to mail.google.com

2.2 User Management: Adding and Removing Users

Now that we have an account working with our domain, it is the perfect time to learn how to add and remove users. First up, you need to access the Admin Controls of your account. You can easily do so by visiting admin.google.com and logging in using your credentials. You will be at your Google Admin Page when you successfully log in. It should look like the image below.

To get started on adding a user, click on the "Add a user."

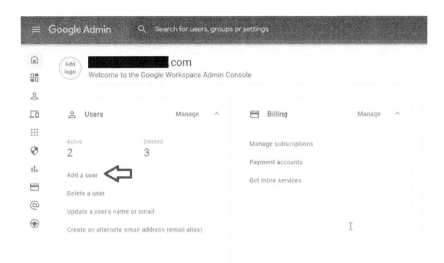

You will be taken to the Add New User page. Here, you are to input the required information, those with the asterisk symbol (*) beside them, which are usually the First name, Last name, and Primary Email.

You should note a Secondary Email and a Phone number that can be added. Although these are not essential for adding a user, it is still best to add these details, for they play a big part in account recovery.

You can manually add the user password or put a profile picture by clicking "Manage user password, organizational unit, and profile photo."

A drop-down box will appear. To add a photo for the user, click "Upload Profile Photo." There are two ways of adding a password: one is by allowing Google to generate a password for the user automatically, and another is to select "Create Password," in which you can manually input a password for the user. When satisfied with the information, click "Add New User" on the bottom right of the page to complete the setup.

If done successfully, you will see a "New user added" message on the top left of the page. Below the profile picture, you can copy the password by clicking "Copy Password" or print the user's information by clicking "Print." Be careful when printing the data since it includes the user's password.

Below this, you will see the "send in sign-in instructions area" where you can email a user, and they can create their password. From here, you can click "Done" when you are finished or select "Add Another User" to add another new user.

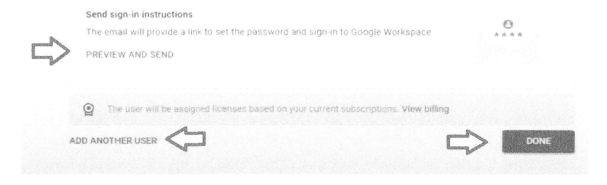

Now that we know how to add users, how do we delete them now that we know how to add users, how do we delete them? In our section, we will look at just that. As always, you will need to log into admin.google.com. In the left corner of the page click on "Directory" and below it selects "Users"

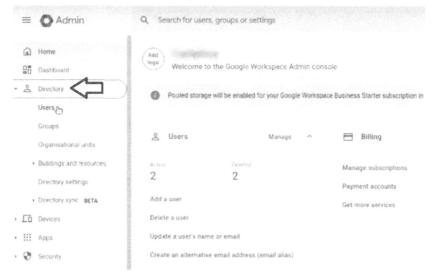

On the User page, you will see a list of users, and you can click on the user's name to access that user's details. If you have a lot of users, use the search bar at the top by typing in their username.

Once you have found the user, you can see the "Delete User" option below on that specific user's detail page, which will start deleting the user.

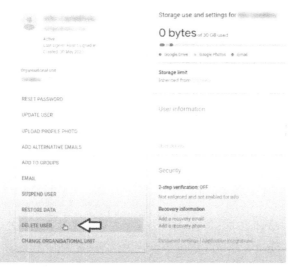

Before deleting the user completely, Google will ask if you want to transfer their data to another user or email or if you want to delete it without transferring at all. Select whatever option suits your needs and then click "Delete user" on the bottom right of the page.

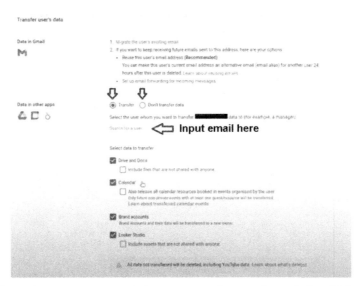

You will be taken back to the user page, and the user you have selected should have been deleted. With that ends the tutorial on adding and deleting users.

2.3 Transitioning from Other Services (To be Updated)

Google Workspace has many competitors, and of course, these competitors offer similar tools and services to their users. There can be some differences based on pricing, quality, interface, and even design. For people interested in switching to Google Workspace, the transition from one service to another may be daunting and prevent them from changing services. So, a familiar question arises. If you are using other productivity suites and then decide to switch to Google Workspace, is it easy?

The short answer is yes, if you utilize one of its rivals, Google Workspace is simple. Thanks to the many connectors that Google Workspace offers with other programs, you may quickly link your Google Workspace account with your other tools.

To access your Gmail inbox and Google Calendar events in Outlook, you can combine Google Workspace with Microsoft Outlook. Additionally, Google Workspace and Salesforce can be connected so that Google Sheets can track your sales leads and opportunities. Additionally, Google Workspace provides several features that can aid in your transition from other productivity suites. For instance, using the Google Workspace Migration Tool, you may transfer your email, contacts, and calendars from Microsoft Exchange to Google Workspace.

Refrain from being concerned about the transition if you are considering converting to Google Workspace but are concerned about it. If you use competitors, Google Workspace makes it simple to utilize. The following are some ways Google Workspace makes it simple to use if you use its rivals:

- The numerous additional programs that Google Workspace connects with make it simple to link your Google Workspace account to your other tools.
- Google Workspace provides several tools that can help and assist you in making the switch from competing productivity suites.
- Google Workspace is thoroughly documented, making it possible to learn how to use it even if you are not familiar with it.
- In case you need customer support, you can contact Google Workspace's 24/7 support team if you need assistance.

Google Workspace is a wonderful alternative to consider if you are looking for a cloud-based productivity suite that is simple to use, even if you utilize other rivals.

3 COMMUNICATION TOOLS

3.1 Gmail

Google created the web-based email service Gmail. It is a free service with several features, such as:

- Gmail filters spam emails using various techniques, so you do not have to worry about an overflowing inbox.
- For virus protection, Gmail checks all incoming emails for viruses and malware.
- Gmail provides free storage of 15 GB, which is sufficient for most users. For additional storage space, you can upgrade to a premium plan.
- Gmail enables you to categorize and manage your emails using labels and filters. You can easily and quickly find the emails you need as a result.
- Gmail's search function is highly robust. Emails can be found using the sender, recipient, subject, or even the email text.
- You can work together on emails in Gmail. This is a fantastic approach to collaborating on projects or imparting knowledge to coworkers.
- Gmail is accessible via mobile apps so you can view your email anywhere.

Gmail is a trustworthy and secure email service that provides several tools to improve the effectiveness and productivity of your email experience. If you want a free email service, Gmail is a fantastic choice.

3.2 Setting Up

To set up a Gmail account is very easy. Visit the website www.gmail.com, and on the bottom of the page, select "Create Account" to get started.

The next page will only require your first name. Your last name is optional, but it is best to provide it. Then click next to continue.

The next page will now ask for your birthday and to provide your gender. Then again, click next when you are done.

The next page will be to choose your Gmail address. You can choose from the premade addresses Google offers or create your own. Once you have decided, then click next.

Next page, you will need to make a password. Make sure to make a strong password using a mix of numbers, small and capital letters, and special characters. Then click next.

You must receive a verification code based on the mobile phone number on the next page. When you receive the text on your phone, please input the verification code on the Google page to continue.

Once you are done, you will add a recovery email. A recovery email is used just in case you cannot access the Gmail account you created, but this is optional.

On the next page, you can register a mobile phone number; Google will use this for account security reasons only.

The next page will be to agree on the Privacy and Terms.

Google

Privacy and Terms

We publish the Google Terms of Service and the YouTube Terms of Service (both of which include information about your 14-day withdrawal right) so that you know what to expect as you use Google services, including YouTube. By choosing 'I agree' you agree to these terms.

A Google Account allows you to access a range of Google services, such as Gmail and Google Drive. An account also offers access to some additional features that require signing in. For example, when you sign in to Google Maps, you can save your "Home" and "Work" addresses. And when you sign in to YouTube, you can like videos, subscribe to channels, and create your own YouTube channel. Google's Terms of Service apply to this list of services, a list that also provides links to service-specific additional terms and policies that explain what you can expect from using Google services, and what we expect from you.

And remember, Google's Privacy Policy describes how Google handles information generated as you use Google services.

You're in control of the data we collect & how it's used

Finally, you are done with creating a Gmail account.

3.3 Advanced Features

Gmail has many features that can help users with their daily email tasks. Let us look at these advanced features that Gmail provides.

Smart Compose

A Gmail feature called Smart Compose uses machine learning to make text suggestions as you type. It can assist you in writing emails more quickly by recommending popular words, salutations, and closings. Although Smart Compose is enabled by default, you can disable it in the Gmail settings. Start an email and utilize Smart Compose from there. Smart Compose will suggest text for you to utilize as you type. The proposal can be accepted by inputting your text or by using the Tab key. As you type, Smart Compose will keep making text suggestions. Although Smart Compose tries its best, occasionally, it may propose inappropriate or inaccurate content.

You can delete any suggestions that you decide not to utilize. Smart Compose can be toggled on or off by going to Settings > See all settings > Compose and respond > Smart Compose to disable it. Delete the check mark next to Smart Compose. Here are some pointers for making the most of Smart Compose:

- When typing, be precise. Smart Compose will more likely propose the appropriate content if you are more explicit.
- Use simple language. Smart Compose has a large vocabulary because it was trained on a large corpus of material. Take advantage of these words and phrases.
- Be tolerant. Because Smart Compose is still being developed, the ideal text may only sometimes be suggested. Erase any suggestions you do not wish to use and continue typing.

Example image of Smart Compose feature in Gmail.

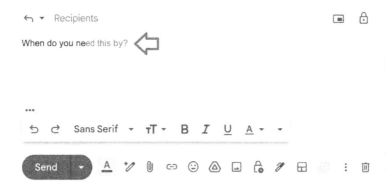

SMART REPLY

Smart Reply is another Gmail feature that employs machine learning to propose quick, pre-written email responses. You can use it to respond to emails rather than typing everything out rapidly. Although Smart Reply is enabled by default, you can disable it in the Gmail settings. Open the email you wish to reply to using Smart Reply. You will see a few suggested responses beneath the email. To submit a recommended reply, click on it or input your own. Smart Reply might suggest better responses, which occasionally makes inappropriate or inaccurate suggestions. You can disregard suggestions that you do not want to use. To turn Smart Reply on or off, you must go to Settings > See all settings > Compose and Reply > Smart Reply to disable it. Delete the check mark next to Smart Reply.

Here are some pointers for making the most of Smart Reply:

- Before selecting a response, thoroughly review the email. Make sure the response is pertinent to the circumstance.
- Be mindful of the email's tone. Smart Reply may suggest excessively informal or formal responses.
- Make good decisions. Refrain from disregarding a suggested response if a correction is necessary.

Additional information regarding Smart Reply is provided below:

- With the help of a sizable dataset of email conversations, Smart Reply is trained to identify common patterns and expressions.
- Since Smart Reply is continuously being updated, it will become better at proposing appropriate responses over time.
- English, French, German, Spanish, Portuguese, Italian, Japanese, Korean, and Chinese are the languages to which Smart Reply is accessible.

Example image of Smart Reply feature in Gmail.

TABBED INBOX

A feature of Gmail called the tabbed inbox separates your inbox into tabs like Primary, Social, Promotions, Updates, and Forums. You can more easily locate the emails you need by organizing your inbox. The Primary tab comprises significant emails from your contacts and websites you have subscribed to. Emails from social media platforms like Facebook and Twitter are found on the social tab. Emails from companies and organizations, including promotional emails, can be found under the Promotions page. Emails from businesses you use, such as your bank or airline, can be found on the Updates tab. Emails from online forums and discussion groups are found under the Forums category.

You may personalize the tabs in your inbox by adding or deleting tabs and modifying their names. The tabs can also be completely hidden if you choose.

Click on the tab you want to view to use the tabbed inbox. The keyboard commands j and k can also jump to the next or previous message. Use the tabbed inbox to arrange your emails and find the ones you need fast. You can always hide it whenever you are not using the tabbed inbox.

Here are some more specifics on the tabbed inbox:

- Both the Gmail app for Android and iOS and Gmail on the web offer tabbed inbox.
- The tabbed inbox has the following default tabs: Primary, Social, Promotions, Updates, and Forums.
- You can add or delete tabs from the tabbed inbox by selecting See all settings from the Settings gear icon in the top right corner. Next, select the tabs you want to display or hide by clicking the Inbox tab.
- By clicking on the tab, you want to rename and entering a new name, you can alter the names of the tabs in the tabbed inbox.
- You can conceal the tabbed inbox by selecting See all settings from the Settings gear icon in the top right corner of the inbox. After that, select the Inbox tab and deselect Tabbed inbox in the pop-up menu.

Example image of Tabbed Inbox feature in Gmail.

NUDGING

Nudging is a subtle method of persuading individuals to perform a particular action. It is frequently used in marketing and persuasion, but it can also be used in education and healthcare.

There are numerous methods to influence people. Some typical scenarios include:

- Defaults are the options selected for individuals if they do not take any action. For instance, a website's default settings may permit cookies to be stored on your computer. Changing the default setting can persuade users to choose otherwise.
- Reminders can be utilized to encourage individuals to act. For instance, a doctor may send a patient a reminder to schedule a follow-up appointment.
- Social norms are unwritten rules governing our conduct. By emphasizing social norms, you can persuade individuals to conform to them.
- Scarcity can be utilized to make something appear more desirable. For instance, a company may offer a limited-time discount to encourage customers to purchase its product before the deal expires.

Nudging is an effective method for influencing people's conduct. However, it must be used with ethics and responsibility. People should not be manipulated or taken advantage of using nudging.

Example image of Nudging feature in Gmail.

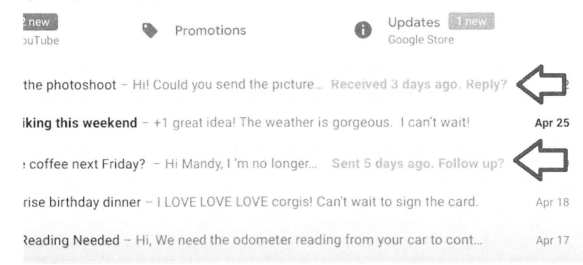

Retract An Already Sent Email

This Gmail feature allows you to retract an already sent email. This can be beneficial if you send an email with an error or change your mind about sending the email. To use Undo, Send, select the Send button and then the Undo button immediately below the message. You will have seconds to cancel the send before sending the message. Depending on your settings, you can cancel the sent message. You have 5 seconds to cancel the send by default. However, this configuration can be modified in the Gmail settings. Go to Settings > See all settings > Undo Send to modify the "undo send" setting. You can then select the number of seconds required to cancel the send. Undo Send is a useful feature that can prevent you from sending regrettable emails. However, it is essential to note that there are superior options available. You cannot reverse the send if the recipient has already opened the email or has a copy in their inbox. Here are some further particulars about Undo Send:

- Undo Send is available in Gmail for the web and Android and iOS Gmail apps.
- Not all email clients support the Undo Send feature. For instance, it is unavailable for organization-managed Gmail accounts.
- Undo Send is not a foolproof method to prevent sending regrettable emails. You cannot reverse the send if the recipient has already opened the email or has a copy in their inbox.

Example image of Undo Send feature in Gmail.

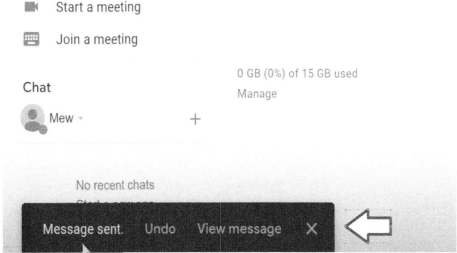

SCHEDULED SEND

6. Scheduled Send is a Gmail feature that enables you to send an email later and later. This can be beneficial if you want to send an email outside of business hours or if you are going to send an email at

a specific time. To schedule an email, compose the message as usual.,. Then, click on the "Send" button and select "Schedule send," where you can select the date and time for the email. The appointed email will be stored in your drafts folder until scheduled delivery. At the specified time, the recipient will receive the email. Additionally, you can schedule an email to be sent multiple times. For instance, schedule a daily email to be sent at 8:00 a.m. Scheduled Send is a useful feature that can help you manage your email more efficiently and save time. Here are some further particulars about Scheduled Send:

- Scheduled Send is available in Gmail for the web and Android and iOS Gmail apps.
- Scheduled emails are sent according to the time zone of the originator.
- It is possible for scheduled emails to be sent a few minutes after the scheduled time.
- At any moment, you can cancel a scheduled email.

Example image of Schedule Send feature in Gmail.

Clicking on the arrow key beside the "Send" button allows you to choose a schedule.

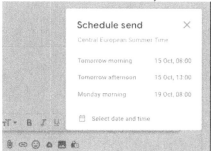

GMAIL'S PRIORITY INBOX

Gmail's Priority Inbox automatically organizes your emails into three categories: Important, Unread Important, and Everything Else. This can help you prioritize the most important emails and swiftly locate the ones you need. The Important category comprises emails that Gmail has deemed to be essential. This is determined by various factors, including the correspondent, the subject line, and the email's keywords. The Important and Unread category comprises important and unread messages. This is a useful method for keeping track of communications requiring follow-up. The Other category comprises all the remaining emails. This section contains communications from newsletters, social media platforms, and other sources. You can modify the Priority Inbox by adding, removing, and renaming existing sections. You can also choose to conceal the Priority Inbox completely.

To utilize the Priority Inbox, select the desired section. You can also use the keyboard shortcuts j and k to navigate to the next and previous messages. Priority Inbox is a helpful email management tool that prioritizes the most essential messages. You can always conceal the Priority Inbox if you are not using it. Here are some further details regarding Priority Inbox:

- Priority Inbox is accessible via Gmail for the web and the Android and iOS Gmail apps.
- Priority Inbox's default sections are Important, Important and Unread, and Everything Else.
- You can add or remove sections by choosing the Settings gear icon in the top-right corner of Priority Inbox and selecting See all settings. Then, pick the Inbox tab and choose the sections to display or conceal.
- You can alter the names of Priority Inbox's sections by clicking on the section you wish to rename and entering a new name.
- You can conceal the Priority Inbox by choosing the Settings gear icon in the upper-right corner of the inbox and selecting See All settings. Then, click the Inbox tab and clear the Priority Inbox checkbox.

Example image of Priority Inbox feature in Gmail.

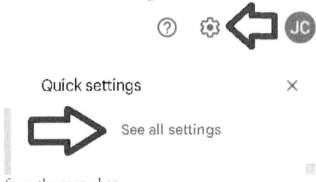

LABELING

8. Labeling in Gmail is a method for organizing communications by subject or project. You can create custom email labels and implement them, as necessary. This can help you quickly locate the emails you need and organize your inbox. Follow these instructions to create a label in Gmail:

1. Click the gear icon in the upper right corner of the inbox to access the Settings menu.
2. Choose View all preferences or See All Settings.

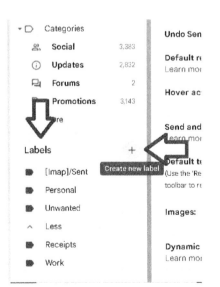

3. Select the Labels tab from the menu bar.
4. Click the icon label creation.

5. Enter the label's name.
6. Simply press the Create icon.

After creating a label, you can attach it to an email by taking the following steps:

1. Open the message you wish to label.
2. Click the Labels button in the upper right corner of the email.
3. Choose the designation you wish to apply for.

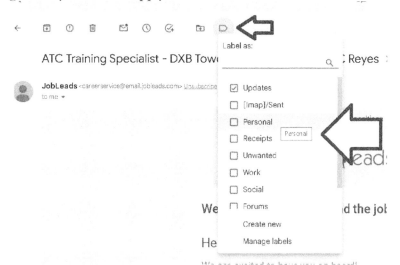

Additionally, you can assign multiple labels to an email. To accomplish this, hold down Ctrl while selecting the labels. Click the Labels tab in the left sidebar of the inbox to view your labels. Additionally, you can filter your labels by name, color, or creation date. Additionally, you can construct a filter in Gmail to automatically label emails based on certain criteria, such as the sender, the subject line, or the keywords in the email. You can visit the Gmail help center to learn more about filters.

Here are some additional Gmail email labeling tips:

- Use labels that authentically reflect the email's content and are descriptive.
- Be consistent with your labeling to locate the necessary emails readily.
- Utilize colors to organize your labeling visually.
- Create a system for labeling your emails so you can easily locate them in the future.

8. Gmail can search your inbox for emails based on keywords, sender, recipient, date, and other criteria. Use the search bar at the top of the inbox to search for emails.

Follow these procedures to locate emails in Gmail:

1 Input the search terms you wish to use in the search bar.

2. Additionally, you can use the following operators to refine your search

- is: unread to search for unread emails
- from:sender to search for emails from a specific sender
- to:recipient to search for emails sent to a specific recipient

- subject:subject to search for emails with a specific subject line
- date:date to search for emails sent on a specific date
- has:attachment to search for emails with attachments

3. Select the Search option.

Gmail will yield a list of emails matching your specific search criteria. The emails can then be opened, deleted, or moved to a different folder.

You can also use the search bar to search for emails in your categories and filters. Before you begin typing your search terms, select the Labels or Filters tab in the left sidebar of the inbox.

Visit the Gmail support center for more information about Gmail search.

Here are a few additional suggestions for using the Gmail search function:
- Utilize specific keywords to avoid receiving excessive results.
- Employ quotation marks to locate precise matches for phrases.
- Use the link for Advanced search to find emails using more complex criteria.
- Utilize the Search history link to view the outcomes of your past queries.

3.4 Security Measures

Google takes Gmail's security very seriously. Gmail dispatches security alerts to notify you of suspicious activity on your account. These alerts can assist you in identifying and addressing security threats swiftly."

TLS encryption

TLS encryption is a security protocol that safeguards the confidentiality and integrity of internet-sent data. Gmail employs it to encrypt all emails sent and received through the service. This indicates that unauthorized parties cannot intercept and view your communications. TLS encryption functions by converting your email into a code only the intended recipient can decode. This code is generated by the sender and recipient using a shared key. When sending an email, the sender encrypts it with the key and transmits it over the internet. When the recipient receives the email, they use the same key to decrypt it. TLS encryption is a highly effective method for safeguarding your communications. In addition to Gmail, it is utilized by many other services, such as HTTPS, which is used to secure websites.

Here are some additional TLS encryption details:
- Transport Layer Security (TLS) is the acronym for Transport Layer Security.
- TLS is a cryptographic protocol that employs asymmetric encryption to secure Internet communications.
- Numerous services, including Gmail, HTTPS, and VPNs, utilize TLS.
- TLS is a highly secure protocol to safeguard sensitive data such as passwords and financial information.

Example image of TLS Encryption feature in Gmail.

Two-factor authentication (2FA)

Two-factor authentication (2FA) is an additional layer of security that requires you to input a code from your phone and your Gmail password. This makes it significantly more difficult for someone to breach your account, even with your password.

To configure 2FA in Gmail, please follow these steps:

1. Navigate to the Gmail settings. Click on your profile picture and select Manage your Google Account, or you can visit https://myaccount.google.com/

2. When you are on your Google Account Page, select the Security option.
3. Click 2-Step Verification in the Signing into Google section after scrolling down.

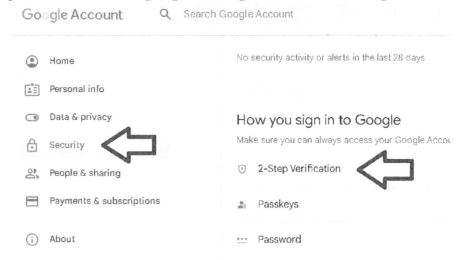

4. Click the Get Started icon to begin.
5. Follow the setup instructions for 2FA.

You must install the Google Authenticator app on your mobile device. After installing the application, you will be given a QR code. Scan the QR code using the Google Authenticator mobile application. The application will then produce a code. Enter the code and select the Verify button in Gmail. Additionally, you will receive a backup code. Keep this code secure if your phone is lost or stolen. When you sign into Gmail from a new device or browser after enabling 2FA, you must input the code from your phone.

Here are some additional Gmail 2FA details:

- MFA is another name for two-factor authentication.
- 2FA is an effective method of preventing unauthorized access to your Gmail account.
- There are additional methods for implementing 2FA, such as using a security token.
- You can also use two-factor authentication with your bank and social media accounts.

Spam And Phishing Filters

The spam and phishing filters in Gmail are intended to protect you from receiving unsolicited emails. Emails containing malevolent content are screened for by spam filters and prevented from reaching the inbox. Emails attempting to fool you into divulging sensitive or personal information, such as your password or credit card number, are identified by phishing filters. Here are several methods in which Gmail's spam and phishing filter's function:

- They examine emails for common spam and phishing-related keywords and phrases.
- They examine email addresses and sender identities for patterns.
- They examine email content for signs of dubious activity.
- They employ machine learning to identify new spam and fraud techniques.

If Gmail's spam or phishing filters mark an email as spam or phishing, it will be sent to the Spam or Phishing tab in your inbox. You can also choose to have these messages deleted automatically.

The efficacy of Gmail's spam and phishing filters is continuously enhanced through regular updates. Nevertheless, no spam or fraud filter is flawless. It is essential always to be vigilant and on the watch for suspicious emails.

Sandboxing

Sandboxing in Gmail is a security feature that isolates messages in a safe environment, preventing them from harming your computer or account. When Gmail receives an email, it is examined for malware. If the email is identified as malicious, it is transferred to a sandbox, a secure environment that can be analyzed without endangering your computer or account. The email is subjected to various tests in the simulator to determine whether it contains malware or other malicious content. If an email is determined to be harmful, it is deleted. If the email is secure, it will be sent to your inbox. The sandboxing feature of Gmail is an essential security feature that protects your computer and account from malicious emails. It is one of the many security measures employed by Gmail to protect your communications.

Here are additional details regarding Gmail's sandboxing:

- Many email service providers employ sandboxing as a security measure.
- Sandboxing provides consumers with protection against malware and other malicious content.
- Sandboxing is an ongoing process that continually adapts to new threats.

5. Gmail's data loss prevention (DLP) features to safeguard your sensitive information from being accidentally sent or deleted. DLP principles can be utilized to identify and prevent sensitive information-containing emails from being sent to unauthorized recipients or deleted.

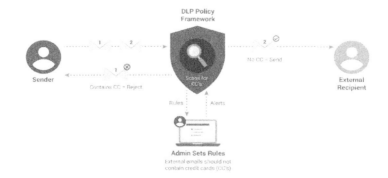

The following are some of the functions of Gmail's DLP features:

- They can scan emails for sensitive information-related keywords and phrases.
- They can be used to identify unauthorized email recipients.
- They can be used to prevent the deletion of communications.

The DLP features of Gmail can be tailored to your specific requirements. You can create your own DLP rules or use the rules that Gmail already has defined.

Here are some guidelines for utilizing the DLP features of Gmail:

- Create DLP protocols to protect the most sensitive data you manage.
- Review your DLP rules frequently and revise them, as necessary.
- Validate the functionality of your DLP principles through testing.

You can safeguard your sensitive data against loss or exposure using Gmail's DLP features.

6. Gmail notifies you of suspicious account activity via security notifications. These alerts can assist you in identifying and addressing security threats swiftly.

Here are some instances of suspect behavior that Gmail may flag:

- Gmail will notify you if someone attempts to access your account from a device or location you do not recognize.
- Changes to your password will trigger an email notification from Gmail.
- If someone transmits many emails to many recipients, Gmail may send you an alert.
- Gmail may send you an alert if you receive an email that appears to be from Google but is fraudulent.

Verify it's you

 @gmail.com

We noticed unusual activity in your Google Account. To keep your account safe, you were signed out. To continue, you'll need to verify it's you.

Continue

If you receive a security alert from Gmail, you must immediately act. You need to:

- Review account activity: Sign in and review your recent actions. Examine any suspicious activity, such as sign-ins from new devices or locations.
- If your password has been changed, you should promptly change it.
- Enable two-step verification: Two-factor authentication (2FA) adds a layer of account security. When two-factor authentication is enabled, you will be required to input a code from your phone in addition to your password when logging in.

By acting when you receive a security alert from Gmail, you can prevent unauthorized access to your account. Here are some additional safety recommendations for using Gmail:

- Utilize a robust password: Your Gmail password should blend uppercase and lowercase letters, numbers, and special characters.
- Never divulge your password: Never disclose your Gmail password, not even with family and friends.
- Use caution when clicking on links. Often, phishing emails contain connections to malicious websites. Be wary of email connections, particularly if you need to recognize the sender.
- Maintain software updates: Google routinely releases Gmail security updates. Ensure that these updates are installed as soon as they become available.

By adhering to these guidelines, you can maintain the security of your Gmail account.

3.5 Google Chat, Hangouts, Spaces

Google's communication tools, Google Chat, Google Hangouts, and Google Chat Spaces, enable you to connect with others.

- Google Chat is a unified messaging application that integrates traditional chat with contemporary features such as video calls and file sharing. It is accessible via the Internet and on Android and iOS devices. Google Chat enables you to communicate with individuals or groups and create spaces designated areas for conversations on topics. Spaces can be made public or private and are utilized for project collaboration, idea sharing, and general discussions. Google Chat integrates with other Google Workspace applications, including Gmail, Docs, and Sheets, making file sharing and project collaboration simple.

  Here are some of Google Chat's most key features:
  - ➢ Communicate with individuals or teams
  - ➢ Create spaces for focused discourse
  - ➢ Share documents and work together on tasks
  - ➢ Compatible with other Google Workspace applications
  - ➢ Web-based, Android, and iOS device compatibility

  Google Chat is a good option for those searching for a secure, dependable, and feature-rich messaging application.

- Google Hangouts is a defunct messaging application that Google Chat superseded. You could communicate with individuals or groups, as well as make video calls, using Hangouts. It was accessible via the Internet and on Android and iOS devices. Integrating Hangouts with other Google Workspace applications, such as Gmail, Docs, and Sheets, facilitates file sharing and project collaboration. Here are some of Google Hangouts' most key features:
  - ➢ Communicate with individuals or teams
  - ➢ Conduct video conversations
  - ➢ Share documents and work together on tasks
  - ➢ Compatible with other Google Workspace applications
  - ➢ Web-based, Android, and iOS device compatibility

  Google Hangouts was a popular messaging application, but Google Chat replaced it. Google Chat offers a wider range of features, including spaces dedicated to conversations about specific topics.

- Google Chat Spaces are a feature of Google Chat that enables organized, topic-specific conversations. Anyone can establish spaces, which can be made either public or private.

  Spaces are comparable to channels in other messaging applications, with a few added features. For instance, spaces can be organized into topics, and users can be @mentioned to draw their attention. Spaces also integrates with other Google Workspace applications like Drive and Docs, facilitating file sharing and project collaboration.
  Here are some of Google Chat Spaces' key features:
  - o Organized and targeted discussions of specific subjects
  - o Both public and restricted areas
  - o Ability to @mention individuals
  - o Compatibility with other Google Workspace applications

  Google Chat Spaces are an excellent platform for project collaboration, idea sharing, and general discussions. Try spaces if you are using Google Chat.
  Here are some additional Google Chat Spaces details:

- Those with a Google Workspace account can create spaces.

- Members are limited to a maximum of 250 per space.
- Spaces can be organized by topic, thereby facilitating the organization of conversations.
- There are both public and private spaces. Public spaces are visible to everyone, whereas private spaces are only visible to members of the space.
- Spaces are compatible with Google Workspace applications such as Drive, Docs, and Sheets. This facilitates file sharing and collaboration on initiatives.

In summary, Google Chat is the successor to Google Hangouts and offers more features, such as spaces.

3.6   Creating Chat Rooms

On the Computer

1. Go to https://mail.google.com/chat

2. Click "**Find a Chat**" or "**Find a Space to join.**"

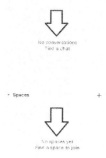

3. Click "**Create a Space**" and enter a name.

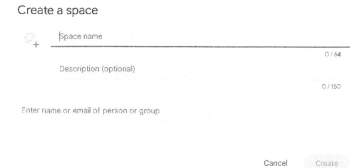

4. Click **Add people & apps.**

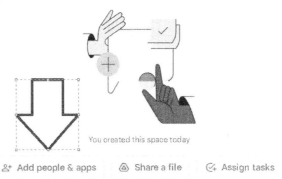

5. Enter names, email addresses, and applications, or choose from the list of suggestions. Include everyone in your organization in suggestions, even if they do not have Hangouts Chat. Repeat for every guest.
6. Click "**Add.**"

You can start chatting with the people you added when you are done.

On Mobile Devices

1. First download and install Google Chat app.

2. Now open Google Chat and ensure you are logged into your account.
3. Click on the "**New Chat**" on the bottom right.

4. On the next page, you need to create a name for your Space, and if you want, you can add an Emoji picture. Once done, click "**Next.**"

5. On the next page, you can add people, but you can skip this process if you also desire to add people later after creating the Space.

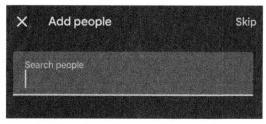

You need to search for those people using the search bar and input their email addresses to add people.

6. Finally, you have created your space; if you have not added anyone, you can do so here. Other things you can do are share files and Assign Tasks.

3.7 Managing Permissions

In Google Chat, there are two methods to manage permissions:
- Permissions for a space determine who can join and administer it.
- Permissions for a chat decide who can view and partake in it.

Space Permissions

In Google Chat, space permissions determine who can join and administer a space. These permissions can be specified by the space's creator or administrator. These permissions can be assigned to each space:
- Who is permitted to attend the space?
- Who can administer the space, including adding or removing members, modifying space settings, and deleting the space.
- Who has access to the message history of a given space.
- Apply @all: Who can use the @all mention to convey a message to the entire space members.

The following are the default permission parameters for a space:
- Anyone in the organization is welcome to participate.
- Only the space's creator can administer the space.
- View message history: Any member of the organization can view the message archive.
- Only the space creator and administrators can use the @all mention.

Changes to space permissions can be made by the space's creator or administrator. To modify space authorization:

1. Click the Settings icon (three dots) in the space's upper-right corner to access its settings.
2. Select Permissions and select the permissions for each user or group using the drop-down menus.
3. Click Save to store your modifications.

Chat Permissions

Google Chat's chat permissions determine who can view and participate in a communication. The chat's creator or administrator can specify these permissions. Each conversation can have the following permissions assigned to it:

- Who has access to the chat.
- Participation: Who can transmit and receive chat messages.

The following are the default permission parameters for a chat:

- Everyone in the organization has access to the chat
- Only chat participants and the chat creator can transmit and receive messages in the chat.

Permission for a chat can be modified by its creator or an administrator. To modify messaging authorization:

1. Launch the chat and select the Settings icon (three dots) in the upper-right corner.
2. Select Permissions and select the permissions for each user or group using the drop-down menus.
3. Click Save to store your modifications.

Here are some additional considerations regarding conversation permissions:

- The chat permissions are distinct from the space permissions. This means that a user can have varying communication permissions.
- Permissions for chat can be modified at any time.
- The chat permissions are applied to all future chat communications. Messages sent before the modification of permissions are unaffected.

3.8 Collaboration Features

Google Chat's many collaboration features make it an effective instrument for working with others.

- Spaces: Spaces are designated locations for specific conversations. They can work together on initiatives, exchange ideas, and participate in general discussions. Spaces can be made public or private and organized by subject matter.
- Google conversation enables users to share files with others within a conversation or space. From your computer, Google Drive, or another cloud storage service, you can share files.
- You can @mention individuals to attract their attention in a chat or shared space. This is an excellent method for notifying someone of a message or posing a query to them.
- Google Chat conversations are threaded, which means that messages are organized into conversations. This makes it simple to track a conversation and view every message sent.
- Emojis can be used to respond to messages in Google Chat. This is an excellent method for expressing approbation, disapproval, or other responses to a message.
- Google Chat provides the ability to search for messages, files, and other content. This is an excellent method for finding the required information.
- Google Chat integrates with other Google Workspace applications including Gmail, Docs, and Sheets. This facilitates file exchange, project collaboration, and the completion of work.

These are some of the collaboration features offered by Google Chat. Google Chat is a great option if you are searching for a robust and flexible collaboration tool.

The following additional collaboration features will shortly be added to Google Chat:

- **Live captions**: Live captions will be available in Google Chat, making it simpler for hard-of-hearing individuals to participate in conversations.
- **Screen sharing**: Screen sharing will be available in Google Chat, facilitating collaboration and the exchange of ideas.
- **Collaboration** on documents: Document collaboration will be available in Google Chat, facilitating real-time collaboration on documents.

These new capabilities will make Google Chat an even more effective collaboration tool.

3.9   Google Voice

Google Voice is a VoIP (Voice over Internet Protocol) service that enables Internet-based phone conversations, text messaging, and voicemail. It is available in the United Kingdom, the contiguous United States, Canada, Denmark, France, the Netherlands, Portugal, Spain, Sweden, and Switzerland.

3.10   Setting Up

Setup for Computers
1. Go to voice.google.com
2. Select if you want to use it "**For Personal use**" or "**For Business**."

3. Search for your city or area code. A list of numbers will populate below. Select one which you wish to use.

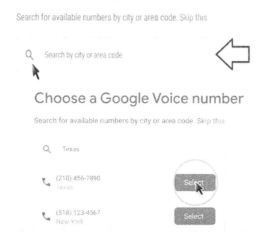

4. Next, you will need to verify using an existing phone number. First, click "**Verify**," and then a popup box will appear. Input the phone number and click "**Send Code**."

5. Another box will pop up, which will ask for the verification code. Click "Verify" when you are done.

6. Once done, you will be directed to the Google Voice homepage and have successfully created your Google Voice number.

Setup for Mobile Devices

1. Download and install the Google Voice App.
2. Sign into your Google account and then accept the terms and conditions of Google Voice located in the lower right of the page.

3. Next enter your phone number.

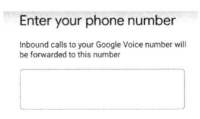

4. Select whether you want to use Google Voice when making a call automatically.

5. Link your account, then allow Voice to access your contacts.

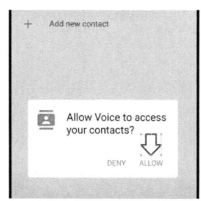

With that, you are all set up and can now start using the Google Voice features on your mobile devices.

3.11 Use Cases and Features

Google Voice connects your phone number to your Google account to function. Using your Google Voice number, you can make and receive phone calls and text messages with any device with a working internet connection. Google Voice also allows you to forward calls to your mobile phone or landline, ensuring that you never miss a call. Google Voice provides numerous features, including:

- Free international calling to other Google Voice users: You can make free international calls to other Google Voice users.
- You can make cheap calls to landlines and mobile phones in the United States and Canada.
- Visual voicemail: You can view a transcript of your voicemails in your inbox, allowing you to readily read them and decide whether to listen to them.
- Call forwarding to another phone number is allowed so that you are always reachable.
- Screen your calls prior to answering to avoid answering unsolicited calls.
- Send and receive text messages using your Google Voice phone number.
- Send group communications to other Google Voice users.
- Receive notifications when you miss a call, allowing you to remain informed about your calls.
- Record your interactions so that you can listen to them later or share them with others.

Here are some additional considerations regarding Google Voice:
- Google Voice telephone numbers are not toll-free.
- Traditional landline and mobile phone calls are not subject to the same quality guarantees as Google Voice calls.
- Google Voice does not support all conventional landline and mobile phone features, such as caller ID and call queuing.

3.12 Financial and Transactional Tools

Google provides various financial and transactional tools that can assist individuals and enterprises in managing their finances. These instruments consist of:

- Google Pay is a mobile payment application that enables you to purchase with your mobile device. Google Pay can be used to pay for products and services in-store, online, and within apps.
- Google Analytics is a analytics service on the web that assists businesses in monitoring and analyzing their website traffic.
- Google Ads is a platform for pay-per-click advertising that enables businesses to display advertisements on Google search results pages and other websites.
- Google Merchant Center is a platform that enables businesses to submit product information to Google for their products to be displayed in Google Shopping results.
- Google Finance is a website that provides real-time information on equities, bonds, currencies, and other financial instruments.

3.13 Google Pay

Google Pay is an online payment system and digital wallet developed by Google. It enables consumers to make in-store, online, and in-app purchases with smartphones. Google Pay transmits payment information between the user's phone and the merchant's point-of-sale (POS) terminal using near-field communication (NFC) technology. Google Pay is accessible in more than two hundred nations and territories. The application supports Credit cards, debit cards, and gift cards. Also supported by Google Pay are loyalty cards, transit passes, and event tickets. Users must establish a Google Pay account and add a payment method to use Google Pay. Once a payment method has been added, consumers can pay with Google Pay. Users must position their phone near the merchant's POS terminal to make a payment. Google Pay will then transmit the payment information to the merchant in a secure manner. Google Pay is a safe and convenient payment method. It is also a contactless payment method, so users do not have to physically present their phone to the merchant when purchasing. Here are a few advantages of using Google Pay:

- Maintaining safety: Google Pay employs the highest security standards in the industry to safeguard your payment information.
- Easily accessible: Google Pay is a contactless payment method allowing fast and easy transactions.
- Millions of merchants around the globe accept Google Pay.
- Integrates with Google's additional services: Google Pay integrates with Google's other services, including Google Maps and Google Assistant. This makes it simple to locate local merchants accepting Google Pay and make voice-activated payments.

You can visit the official Google Pay website at pay.google.com

3.14 Google Analytics

Google offers the web analytics service Google Analytics, which monitors and reports website traffic. It is a freemium service, meaning fundamental features are free, but advanced features cost money. Google Analytics can be used as a monitoring tool for several website traffic metrics:

- Pageviews: The number of times a page has been viewed on your website.
- Unique visitors are the distinct individuals who have visited your website.
- Bounce rate: Monitors the number of visitors who abandon your website after viewing only one page.
- Average time on page: The average amount of time that website visitors spend on each page.
- Conversion rate is the proportion of site visitors who perform the desired action, such as purchasing or subscribing to a newsletter.

Google Analytics is also used to monitor the performance of your marketing campaigns, including search engine optimization (SEO) and pay-per-click (PPC) advertising. It does require you to create a Google Analytics account and upload a tracking code to your website to use Google Analytics. The tracking code will gather your website's traffic information and submit it to Google Analytics. Google Analytics is a potent instrument for monitoring and understanding your website's traffic. Additionally, it can assist you in enhancing your website and marketing campaigns. Here are some advantages of utilizing Google Analytics:

- Free of charge: Google Analytics' fundamental features are free to use.
- Google Analytics can track a variety of website traffic metrics.
- Google Analytics is easy to install and operate.
- Google Analytics is a dependable instrument utilized by millions of businesses.
- Google Analytics can be scaled to suit your organization's needs.

You can visit the official Google Pay website at analytics.google.com

3.15 Google Ads

Google Ads is a pay-per-click (PPC) advertising platform that permits businesses to display their advertisements on the results of Google's search engine and other websites. Google Ads enables businesses to bid on pertinent product and service keywords. Google will display the business's ad if it has the highest bid when someone searches for one of the keywords. Cost per click (CPC) refers to the amount paid for each click on an advertisement. Several factors, including the keyword's competitiveness and the ad's content, determine CPC. Google Ads is a well-known advertising platform utilized by businesses of all sizes. It is an efficient method for reaching a large audience and generating leads or sales. Here are a few advantages of using Google Ads:

- Attain a wide audience: Your Google Ads advertisements can be displayed on Google's search engine results pages (SERPs) and other websites, allowing them to reach a large audience.
- You may target your ads, demographics, and interests using specific keywords so that only people likely to be interested in what you offer see them.
- Google Ads provides comprehensive reports on the performance of your ads so you can monitor their effectiveness and make any necessary adjustments.
- Only pay when a user clicks: You only pay when someone clicks on your ad, so you do not have to stress about wasting money on ineffective impressions.

Google Ads is an excellent choice to reach and influence a large audience while generating leads or sales. Here are some examples of various Google Ads campaigns:

- Display ads: This is the most prevalent form of Google Ads campaign. Your ads will appear at the top of search engine results pages when a user queries for a keyword for which you have bid.
- Display advertisements appear on Google Display Network websites. The Display Network may consist of thousands to millions of websites, allowing your promotions to reach a vast audience.
- These advertisements are on known streaming sites like YouTube, Twitch, and other video-sharing websites. These sites help promote your products and services or to convey your brand's story.
- These advertisements appear on the Shopping tab of Google. They display product information such as price, availability, and images.
- These advertisements promote your mobile applications. They may also appear on other websites, including the Google Play Store.

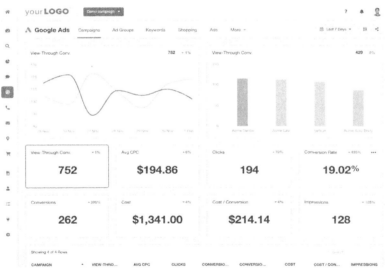

Google Ads is a complex platform, but it can be a helpful service for achieving your market objectives and reaching your target audience. If you are new to Google Ads, you should begin with a small budget and progressively increase it as you gain experience with the platform and how to optimize your campaigns. You can visit the official Google Pay website at ads.google.com

3.16 Google Merchant

Google Merchant Center is a free service that enables businesses to administer their Google Shopping product listings. It is a crucial component of any online retail strategy, allowing businesses to expose their products to more prospective consumers.

Businesses must establish a Merchant Center account and submit product listings to Google Merchant Center. The listings will then be crawled by Google Merchant Center and available on Google Shopping.

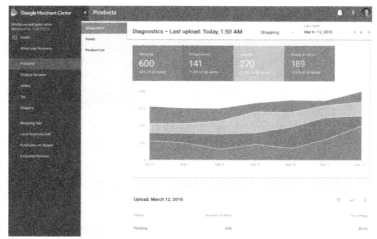

Google Merchant Center provides businesses with a variety of tools to enhance their online sales, including:

- Product feed management: Google Merchant Center allows businesses to administer product feed files containing product information.
- Product Insights: Google Merchant Center provides businesses with information regarding the performance of their products on Google Shopping.
- Google Merchant Center provides businesses with comprehensive reports on their product listings' efficacy.
- Google Merchant Center offers fraud protection to assist businesses in defending themselves against fraudulent transactions.

Google Merchant Center is a useful resource for companies of all sizes. It can help businesses increase online sales by exposing their products to more potential customers.

3.17 Google Finance

Google Finance is a website that provides real-time information on equities, bonds, currencies, and other financial instruments. It is a free utility that anyone can access.

Google Finance includes the following features:

- Google Finance offers real-time quotes for equities, bonds, currencies, and other financial instruments.
- Google Finance provides news and analysis regarding the most recent financial developments.
- Google Finance enables users to keep track of their investment portfolios.
- Google Finance provides research tools to help consumers make informed investment decisions.
- Google Finance provides tools to assist users in managing their finances.

Google Finance is valuable for investors, financial professionals, and anyone seeking the most recent financial news and data.

4   CONTENT & MEDIA MANAGEMENT

Content and media management involves creating, storing, organizing, distributing, and collaborating content and media. It is a vital function for all businesses, big or small, enabling them to effectively manage their intellectual property, communicate with their audiences, and achieve their business goals. There are numerous tools and technologies available for content and media management. Among the most frequent are:

- Cloud-based storage solutions enable organizations to store their content and media assets in a centralized location, making them simple to access and share.
- Using collaboration tools, Multiple users can collaborate to work simultaneously on the same content and media assets.
- CMS: Content management systems These systems provide a comprehensive platform for creating, administrating, and publishing content.
- MAM systems are designed to manage media files such as recordings and photographs.

The tools and technologies utilized for content and media management will vary depending on the organization's requirements. Nonetheless, all organizations should have a method for managing their content and media assets. This procedure should be designed to maintain the safety, security, and accessibility of the content and media. Here are a few advantages of efficient content and media management:

- Most Businesses want to save time and resources, so an effective, well-defined procedure for managing content and media is important.
- Businesses can increase productivity by making it simple for users to locate and access the required content and media.
- Businesses can enhance communication and teamwork by providing tools for collaboration.
- Improved security: By implementing security measures, businesses can secure their content and media from unauthorized access.
- Businesses can reduce the likelihood of non-compliance by implementing a process for managing content and media.

Effective content and media management is crucial for organizations of all sizes. Businesses can improve their efficacy, productivity, collaboration, security, and compliance by instituting a sound process for managing their content and media assets.

4.1   Google Drive

Google Drive is a storage and synchronization service using cloud-based technology that enables users to store and access files online from anywhere. It is part of the suite of Google Workspace productivity applications.

Google Drive provides numerous characteristics, including:

- Google Drive offers consumers 15 GB of free storage space for files. If required, users can purchase additional storage space.
- Synchronization of files: Google Drive synchronizes files across all devices, including computers and mobile devices, and allows users to gain access to their files, even when offline.
- Google Drive facilitates the exchange of files with others. You can share assets with specific individuals or make them accessible to everyone.
- Google Drive facilitates real-time collaboration on files. Multiple users can gain permission to edit the same file simultaneously.
- Google Drive provides several security features to safeguard your files, including two-factor authentication and data encryption.
- Google Drive allows you to preview most file types without downloading them.

- Google Drive has a powerful search function that allows you to locate files swiftly and easily.
- Google Drive lets users create folders and subfolders to help organize their files more efficiently.
- Permissions for file sharing: Google Drive lets you manage who can view and edit your files.
- Google Drive maintains track of all file changes, permitting you to revert to a previous version whenever required.
- Offline file access: Google Drive provides offline file access.
- Google Drive offers mobile applications for iOS and Android devices.

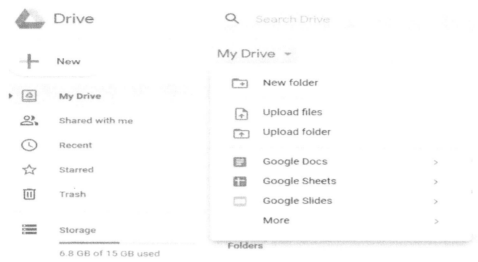

Google Drive is a prominent file storage and synchronization service utilized by individuals and businesses. It is a trustworthy and secure method for storing files and collaborating with others. Here are a few advantages of using Google Drive:

- Google Drive is available from any location with an internet connection.
- Google Drive facilitates real-time collaboration, allowing multiple users to edit the same file concurrently.
- Google Drive has two-factor authentication and data encryption to secure your files.
- Google Drive offers a complimentary plan that includes 15 GB of storage space. If required, users can purchase additional storage space.
- Google Drive integrates with several other Google Workspace applications and third-party applications.

If you are looking for a dependable, secure, and cost-effective method to store your files and collaborate with others, I highly suggest Google Drive. To access Google Drive, visit the website drive.google.com and log into your Google account.

4.2 Google One

Google One is a cloud storage service with greater storage space than Google Drive's complimentary plan. It also incorporates several additional features, including:

- You can share your Google One storage space with up to five family members.
- You can share files with others and determine who has access to view and edit them.
- You can search for files by their name, content, and even the date they were created or modified.
- Restoring discarded files from the trash is possible for up to 30 days.
- You can back up your photos, videos, and files to Google One to access them from anywhere.
- You can back up your Android devices to Google One to restore them if lost or damaged.

Google One is a paid subscription service that offers a complimentary trial—starting at $1.99 monthly for 100 GB of storage space.

Consider this option if you need more storage space for your Google Drive files or want to take advantage of Google One's other features. Here are a few advantages of using Google One:

- Google One provides more storage space than Google Drive's complimentary plan.
- You can share your Google One storage space with up to five family members.
- You can share files with others and determine who has access to view and edit them.
- You can search for files by their name, content, and even the date they were created or modified.
- Restoring discarded files from the trash is possible for up to 30 days.
- You can back up your photos, videos, and files to Google One to access them from anywhere.
- You can back up your Android devices to Google One to restore them if they are lost or damaged.

Google One is a good option if you seek a dependable and secure method to store your files and take advantage of additional features. To access Google One, visit the website one.google.com and log in using your Google account.

4.3 Google Vault

Google Vault is an electronic discovery utility tool used for archiving that can back up and preserve your Gmail messages, Drive files, and other Google Workspace information. It can be used to comply with e-discovery requests, investigate potential legal issues, and store vital information for the long term. Google Vault permits users to:

- Create retention policies to specify the length of time distinct data types should be retained.
- Search for archived data. Using keywords, dates, and other criteria, search for archived data.
- You can export archived data in various formats, including PDF, CSV, and PST.
- You can control who has access to archived data by managing permissions.

Google Vault is an effective tool for managing and securing your Google Workspace data. Organizations that must comply with e-discovery requests, investigate potential legal issues, or retain vital information for long-term storage should consider this option. Here are a few advantages of using Google Vault:

- Google Vault facilitates compliance with e-discovery requests and other regulatory requirements.
- Google Vault can help you investigate potential legal issues by supplying access to archived data.
- Google Vault can assist with the long-term storage of crucial data.
- Google Vault is a secure solution that protects your data with industry-standard encryption.
- Google Vault is a cost-effective solution that enterprises of all sizes can utilize.

To gain access to Google Vault just visit the website vault.google.com

4.4 Google Takeout

Google Takeout is a service that enables you to obtain a copy of your Google data, such as Drive files, Gmail messages, and Calendar events. Google Takeout allows you to back up your data, transfer it to another service, or view it offline.

Google Takeout makes it possible to:

- Select the data to download: You can download all your data or specific categories of data, such as your Drive files or Gmail messages.
- You can download your data in various formats, including ZIP, HTML, and XML.
- You can schedule a download to take place later.
- You can manage downloads by halting, continuing, or deleting them.

Google Takeout is a practical method for backing up your Google data. People who want to keep their data accessible and secure should consider using this tool. Here are some advantages of utilizing Google Takeout:

- Google Takeout makes it simple to back up your Google information with just a few keystrokes.
- Google Takeout employs industry-standard encryption to safeguard your data during the download process.
- Google Takeout lets you obtain your data in various formats, making it simple to import into another service.
- Google Takeout gives you control over the data you download and the time you download it.

Google Takeout is a good option if you want a convenient and secure method to back up your Google data. Visit the website takeout.google.com to gain access to this handy service.

4.5 Google Cloud Storage

Google Cloud Storage is an object storage service that exhibits scalability and durability, providing users with high availability and low latency. Utilizing this storage solution proves advantageous for retaining substantial volumes of data, encompassing multimedia content such as photographs, videos, and backup files.

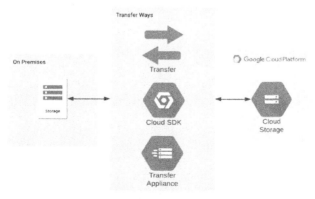

Google Cloud Storage provides a diverse range of functionalities, encompassing:
- Scalability is a prominent feature of Google Cloud Storage since it allows for the flexible expansion of storage capacity to accommodate varying data volumes, ranging from a few gigabytes to petabytes.
- Durability: Google Cloud Storage has been meticulously engineered to exhibit exceptional durability, with an availability service level agreement (SLA) of 99.999999999%.
- Google Cloud Storage provides a low latency feature that enables users to retrieve their data swiftly.
- Google Cloud Storage is equipped with a range of data protection measures, including encryption and access restriction, ensuring high security.
- Cost-effectiveness is a key aspect of Google Cloud Storage, as it offers a wide range of price options that can be tailored to accommodate each user's budgetary requirements.

Google Cloud Storage can serve various functions, encompassing but not limited to:
- Google Cloud Storage can efficiently store substantial quantities of photographs and videos, making it suitable for applications such as website hosting or video streaming services.
- As an effective backup solution, Google Cloud Storage can securely store and safeguard many types of data, including corporate files and personal images.
- Google Cloud Storage can be a hosting platform for static websites, such as blogs or portfolios.
- Google Cloud Storage can efficiently store and process large volumes of data, such as machine learning or analytics datasets.

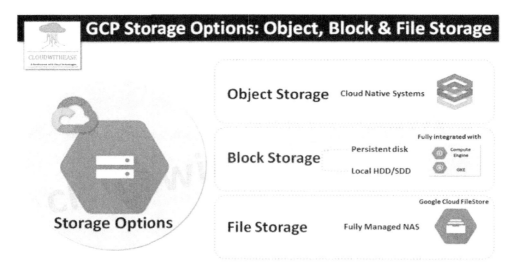

Google Cloud Storage is highly recommended for anyone seeking a scalable, resilient, and fortified object storage solution. The following information provides supplementary details regarding Google Cloud Storage:
- Google Cloud Storage provides a range of storage types, each possessing distinct attributes and cost structures.
- The replication process in Google Cloud Storage involves duplicating data across many regions and zones, serving as a protective measure against potential outages.
- View management is a feature provided by Google Cloud Storage that enables users to manage and regulate the individuals or entities granted permission to view their data.

To view more details on Google Cloud Storage, visit cloud.google.com.

4.6   Google Photos

Google Photos is a digital platform provided by Google that facilitates the storage and distribution of photos and videos. This platform enables users to securely save, efficiently manage, seamlessly edit, and conveniently share various visual media, including images and videos, through an online interface. Google Photos is accessible across multiple devices, encompassing personal computers, smartphones, and tablets. Google Photos provides a diverse range of functionalities, encompassing:

- Google Photos provides users with the opportunity to have unlimited storage for images and movies if they adhere to certain specifications. Specifically, the storage applies to media files with a maximum resolution of 16 megapixels for photos and 1080p for videos. This implies that users can keep unlimited photographs and movies without concerns about storage limitations.

- Google Photos provides an automated backup feature that ensures the preservation of users' photographs and videos by securely storing them in the cloud, thereby mitigating the risk of data loss. This method effectively safeguards one's images and videos against inadvertent deletion or potential harm.

- Google Photos provides diverse capabilities to facilitate the organization of users' photos and videos. These features encompass facial recognition, location tagging, and the creation of albums. This feature facilitates the process of locating desired photographs and movies.

- Google Photos has various editing options that enable users to enhance their photographs and videos. These features include cropping, rotating, and altering the color and contrast of the visual content. This feature facilitates the production of aesthetically pleasing photographs and films.

- The sharing capabilities of Google Photos facilitate the convenient dissemination of personal photographs and movies to others through many channels, including email, text messaging, and social networking platforms. This method provides an excellent means of disseminating personal recollections to acquaintances and relatives.

Google Photos is a widely utilized photo and video storing and sharing platform with significant popularity among individual users and organizations of various scales. The storage and sharing of photographs and videos through this method is dependable and secure. The following information provides more details regarding Google Photos:

- The following are compatible with Google Assistant: Google Photos is compatible with Google Assistant, enabling users to employ voice commands for managing their photographs and videos. As an illustration, one may request, "Google, kindly display images of my feline companion." Google Photos provides a comprehensive display of all the photographs captured by the user, including their feline companion.

- Google Photos offers a range of security measures to safeguard users' photographs and videos, including encryption and two-factor authentication. This implies that the user's pictures and videos are protected against unwanted access.

- Google Photos offers a no-cost option for basic usage. Users can save a maximum of 15 gigabytes (GB) of photographs and movies without incurring costs. If there is a requirement for increased storage capacity, it is possible to get supplementary storage plans.

Google Photos is a commendable choice for anyone seeking a dependable, secure, and user-friendly platform for storing and sharing their photographs and videos. Google Photos is easily accessed by visiting the website at photos.google.com or downloading the application on your mobile device via Google Play Store.

4.7   Google Play Store

The Google Play Store is an internet-based platform for distributing and developing digital content owned and administered by Google—The platform functions as the designated application marketplace for Android devices. The platform provides a diverse range of applications, games, music, movies, books, and additional forms of material. The Android Market was initially introduced in October 2008 and rebranded as Google Play in 2012. As of 2023, the app store has a vast collection of over 3.5 million applications readily accessible for download. Furthermore, it has established itself as the foremost app shop among users of Android smartphones, garnering significant popularity.

The availability of the Google Play Store spans more than 190 nations and territories, with support for over 40 languages. The platform for app downloads is designed with robust security measures, ensuring a safe environment for users. Prior to their distribution on the platform, all apps undergo a thorough screening process conducted by Google. To access and download applications from the Google Play Store, it is necessary to own an Android device and a Google account. After successfully creating an account, users can navigate through the app store and locate applications they desire to download. Users have the option to search for applications based on keywords or categories. After selecting the desired application, hit the "Install" button. Subsequently, the application will be downloaded onto your device.

The Google Play Store provides users with a wide range of functionalities aimed at assisting, locating, and acquiring applications, encompassing the following:

- Application recommendations: The Google Play Store provides app suggestions by leveraging user interests and historical usage patterns, then provides applications that are related to the user.
- One can do a search for applications based on keywords or categories.
- The option to peruse ratings and reviews provided by fellow users is available prior to downloading an application.
- The feature of viewing screenshots of applications before downloading them is available.
- App descriptions provide users with the opportunity to acquire comprehensive information about an application prior to its download.
- In-app purchases refer to the availability of supplementary features or content within some applications that users have the option to acquire through monetary transactions.
- The feature of family sharing allows for the sharing of applications among members of a family unit.
- Subscriptions enable users to avail themselves of applications or services, such as Netflix or Spotify, by enrolling in a recurring payment plan.

In addition to its primary functions, the Google Play Store provides a diverse range of supplementary features, including:

- The Google Play Pass is a subscription-based service that provides users with a carefully curated assortment of applications and games, free from advertisements and in-app purchases.
- Google Play Points is an incentivized program offered by Google that incentivizes users to engage in activities such as app downloads, purchases, and other related actions.
- The utilization of Google Play Gift Cards enables users to acquire various digital content such as applications, games, movies, music, and books from the Google Play Store.

The Google Play Store is a complete digital platform that facilitates downloading various applications, games, music, movies, books, and other multimedia material. Obtaining desired content on an Android device through this method is both secure and efficient.

The utilization of the Google Play Store offers several advantages.

- Convenience: The Google Play Store facilitates the effortless discovery and acquisition of applications, games, music, movies, books, and various other forms of digital material. Users can navigate through the app store by utilizing category- or keyword-based search methods. Before downloading an application, users are allowed to peruse ratings and reviews submitted by fellow users.
- The security measures implemented by Google for the Google Play Store involve a comprehensive review process wherein all applications undergo evaluation and scrutiny prior to

their release. Additionally, these applications are subjected to rigorous scanning procedures to detect and prevent the presence of malware and other forms of dangerous content.

- Diversity: The Google Play Store offers a broad range of content encompassing games, productivity applications, social media platforms, music, movies, books, and further offerings.
- The Google Play Store has a feature that enables automatic updates for applications installed on your smartphone, ensuring that you consistently have the most up-to-date versions of your programs.
- Justification: If users encounter any difficulties with an application, they can seek assistance from Google Play support.

The Google Play Store is a viable choice for individuals seeking a secure, user-friendly, and extensive platform to get applications, games, music, movies, books, and other material specifically tailored for Android devices.

4.8   Google TV

Google TV is a Smart television operating system developed by the technology company Google. The system is built upon the Android TV platform and utilizes the identical foundational operating system. Nevertheless, the software incorporates a novel user interface with enhanced user-friendliness and intuitive design principles. The user interface is developed on Google's discovery engine and employs machine learning techniques to provide personalized content recommendations based on user interests. Google TV is accessible on various intelligent television models Sony, TCL, and Hisense manufactured. Additionally, it can be accessed on Chromecast with Google TV streaming device. The following are a few characteristics of Google TV:

- Individualized suggestions: Google TV utilizes machine learning algorithms to better supply the user with personalized recommendations based on their preferences and interests. The algorithm considers the user's viewing history, their content ratings, and the viewing habits of their friends and relatives.
- Google TV seamlessly incorporates many streaming services, like YouTube, Netflix, and Disney+, into its platform. Additionally, it can seamlessly integrate with various other streaming platforms, like Hulu, Amazon Prime Video, and HBO Max. This feature lets users conveniently access their preferred content from several streaming platforms under a unified interface.
- The utilization of voice search enables users to locate desired material on Google TV. Kindly request Google to display fantasy movies or inquire about the current programming on HBO Max, and Google TV will promptly retrieve the desired content.
- Google TV can stream live television content from a range of sources, including but not limited to YouTube TV, Hulu + Live TV, and Sling TV. This feature enables users to conveniently view their preferred live television programs and athletic events without the need to switch between different input sources.
- Children's Profiles: It is possible to generate profiles specifically designed for children, which limits their access to specific types of content. This method effectively guarantees that youngsters exclusively consume stuff that is suitable for their age group.
- The ambient mode feature of Google TV allows for displaying artwork or photographs during periods of inactivity. This method presents an effective means of imbuing one's television with a sense of individuality and enhancing its aesthetic appeal during periods of non-utilization.

Google TV is a novel and pioneering operating system designed specifically for intelligent television sets. This design aims to enhance the accessibility and convenience of locating and viewing desired material. Google TV is a viable choice for anyone seeking a new smart television. The utilization of Google TV offers several advantages.

- Convenience is a notable feature of Google TV since it facilitates the effortless discovery and consumption of desired content. Users have the option to navigate through material either by category or keyword, and they also can utilize voice search functionality for content retrieval.
- The Google TV platform employs personalized content recommendations by leveraging individual watching history and various other characteristics to provide material that aligns with user preferences. Consequently, there is a reduced probability of spending time perusing material that aligns differently with one's personal interests.
- Integration: Google TV is designed to seamlessly incorporate several Google services, including YouTube, Netflix, and Disney+. Enabling this feature allows users to access their preferred content from several streaming platforms under a unified interface. This feature has the potential to optimize efficiency and reduce the cognitive load associated with locating desired video content.

If one is seeking a technologically advanced television that offers user-friendly navigation and diverse functionalities, Google TV presents itself as a viable choice.

5   DOCUMENT & FILE CREATION

5.1   Google Docs

Google Docs is a web-based word-processing application that forms an integral component of the Google Drive suite of productivity applications. The service is provided at no cost and enables users to generate, modify, and engage in collaborative efforts on various documents. Google Docs is accessible on a wide range of popular web browsers and devices. The following are a few characteristics of Google Docs:

- Collaboration is facilitated by using Google Docs, enabling individuals to engage in real-time collaborative work. This feature enables multiple users access to a shared document for collaboration in real-time, allowing them to make simultaneous edits and observe each other's modifications as they occur. Collaborating with peers or seeking constructive criticism can be an effective approach to engaging in project-based endeavors.
- The version history feature in Google Docs allows for the comprehensive tracking of all modifications made to a document. This feature will enable users to revert to a previous version of a document whenever necessary. This method provides an effective means of monitoring one's progress and rectifying inadvertent alterations.
- Google Docs provides users with diverse formatting choices encompassing various fonts, colors, and styles. This feature lets users personalize their papers according to their preferred visual appearance.
- Google Docs facilitates incorporating photos and tables into documents, simplifying users' tasks. This feature can enhance the visual aspects and facilitate the organization of data.
- Google Docs offers a comprehensive suite of tools that includes an integrated spell-checking and grammar-checking feature. This feature can assist in identifying and rectifying document mistakes prior to their dissemination to others.
- Google Docs have access to cloud storage, which refers to the practice of storing documents in a remote server infrastructure, also known as the cloud, which enables users to access their papers from any location conveniently. This feature is highly advantageous for individuals seeking to collaborate on their projects across several devices or for those requiring seamless sharing capabilities.
- Mobile applications: Mobile applications are designed specifically for utilizing Google Docs, enabling users to work on their projects using their smartphones or tablets conveniently. This

feature is highly advantageous for individuals who require the ability to edit their documents while being mobile.

- Google Docs is a highly capable and adaptable word-processing tool that is both cost-free and user-friendly. Additionally, it offers collaboration features, making it an excellent choice for individuals seeking a comprehensive solution.

Google Docs is a very capable and adaptable word-processing tool that is well-suited for a wide range of tasks, such as generating comprehensive reports, composing scholarly articles, and facilitating collaborative efforts on diverse projects. The collaborative word processor is an excellent choice for individuals seeking a cost-free and user-friendly solution. Visit docs.google.com to start using Google Docs.

5.2 Google Docs – The Basics

This section provides the user with an instructional guide on utilizing Google Docs and its functionalities.

- Create a document: To initiate the creation of a new document, navigate to the website docs.google.com, log in to your Google Account, and proceed by selecting "Blank Page" to create a new blank document.

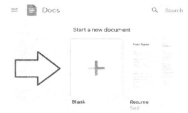

- After creating a new document, the user may proceed to input their desired text.
- The text can be formatted by utilizing the toolbar at the document's upper section. Users can modify several aspects of their text, such as the font, size, color, and style.

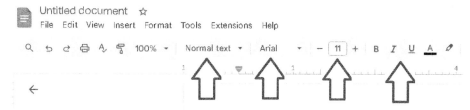

- Inserting photos and creating tables in your document involves using the "Insert" button and selecting the desired element type.

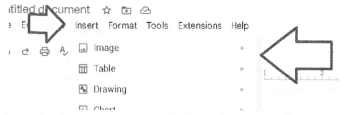

- To provide feedback on the document, please click the "Comment" button or press the shortcut key Ctrl + Alt + M and enter your opinion in the ensuing text box.

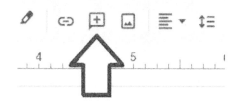

- To monitor modifications to your document, users can select the desired version from the Version history timeline to access the changes made to a particular version. This action will trigger a preview display showcasing the contents of that specific version. This feature will display a comprehensive record of all modifications made to the document, providing details such as the identity of the individuals responsible for the changes and the respective timestamps indicating when these alterations were implemented.

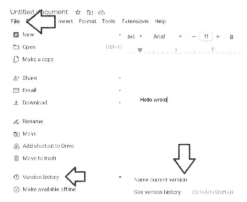

- Google saves your modifications as you type when you're online. A save icon is not required. You can configure offline access to save your changes if you're not connected to the Internet.

- Google Doc can be for offline use by using but if you do so you will have to manually save by going to "File" and click "Save."

  Here are steps to making a document in Google Docs offline:
  Select "File" and scroll down and select "Make available for offline" option.

- To download your document, please use the "File" button and proceed to select the "Download" option.

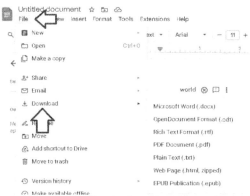

Below are many supplementary suggestions for effectively using Google Docs:

- Utilize keyboard shortcuts as a time-saving measure. Google Docs offers a wide range of keyboard shortcuts that can effectively enhance productivity by reducing time consumption. As an illustration, the user may utilize the keyboard shortcut Ctrl+C to copy text from the document or Ctrl+A to highlight all the text within the document.

- Utilize templates to expedite the initial stages of a project. Google Docs provides a diverse selection of templates that can be readily utilized to initiate tasks expeditiously. One can utilize a standardized format for various documents such as a curriculum vitae, correspondence, or a visual presentation.

- Make use of the search function to locate the desired information or resources. The search box can locate precise textual content or formatting within your document.

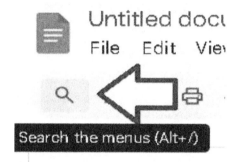

5.3   Real-Time Editing

Google Docs facilitates editing in real-time. This means that multiple individuals can edit the same document simultaneously, and everyone will see the changes in real-time. This facilitates collaboration on documents, even when individuals are not in the same location.

Follow these steps to enable real-time editing in Google Docs:

- Launch the document in which you wish to collaborate.
- Click the "Share" button in the document's upper right corner.

- In the Share dialogue box, enter the email addresses of the individuals with whom you desire to share the document.

- Select Settings and make sure that "Editors can change permissions and share" option is checked.

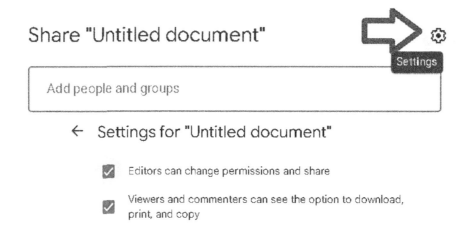

- An alternative is to set the restricted status under General Access by allowing the "Anyone with a link" option. Copy and send the link to the individuals using the copy link option.

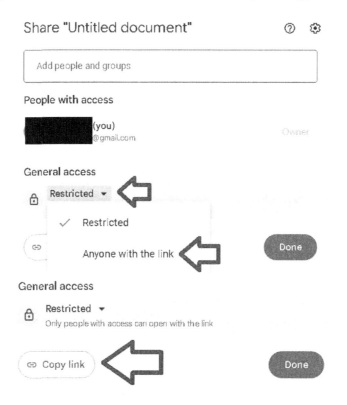

- Click Done.

The individuals you shared the document with can open and edit it immediately. You will be able to see their cursors in the document and their modifications as they are made.

Here are some additional considerations regarding real-time editing in Google Docs:

- A text segment can only be edited concurrently by one person. If two individuals attempt to edit the same section of text simultaneously, their changes will be merged.
- By examining the emblems in the document's upper right corner, you can determine who is editing the document.
- You can contribute comments to the document to provide other collaborators with feedback.
- You can monitor document changes to determine who made what changes and when.

Real-time editing is a potent feature that can facilitate document collaboration with others. If you need to collaborate with multiple individuals on a document, I recommend using Google Docs. Here are some additional guidelines for using Google Docs' real-time editing:

- Utilize @-mentions to alert other collaborators when you refer to them in a comment or modification.
- Use the Comments feature to provide other collaborators feedback without modifying the document.
- Use the Version History feature to monitor changes to the document and, if necessary, revert to an earlier version.

5.4   Templates and Design

Google Docs has a great selection of templates for creating resumes, letters, reports, and presentations, among other document types. You can also discover templates for more specialized tasks, such as writing a resume, writing a letter, designing a website, or writing a book. To locate a template, launch Google Docs and click the "Template gallery" button in the upper left corner of the screen. Then, you can examine the templates by category or conduct a search for a particular template.

Once you have located a suitable template, click on it to access it. The template can then be modified to suit your requirements. You can modify the template's text, typefaces, and colors, among other elements. If you want to construct a custom template, you can begin with a blank document and add your own content and format. After creating your template, you can save it for future use. Here are the steps for making your own custom template.

- Go to "File" and select make "Make a copy" option.

- A box will pop up. In that box, under the Folder section, click the folder.

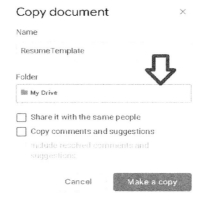

- Create a new folder by clicking on the "New Folder" icon.

- Name the new folder "Custom Template" and click the "Check" Button just to the right of it. Once done, click "Select."

- It will head back to the previous box. Now, click "Make a Copy," and you are done. You can use that copy as a template. Just make sure to make a copy of it so that it will not overwrite the existing template.

Here are a few design suggestions for your Google Docs documents:

- Employ a straightforward and concise format.
- Utilize the same font and font size throughout the entire document.
- Utilize color and imagery to add visual appeal.
- Make the text easier to comprehend by incorporating headings and subheadings.
- Before sharing your document with others, you should proofread it thoroughly.

Here are some of Google Docs' most popular templates:

- This template can assist you in developing a professional resume to present to prospective employers.
- This letter template can be used to construct formal or informal letters.
- This template will assist you in producing a well-organized and informative report.
- The template will assist you in creating a visually enticing and engaging presentation.
- This template can help you construct a simple website without coding knowledge.
- This template will assist you in writing a book in Google Docs.

5.5   Google Sheets

Google Sheets is an online web-based spreadsheet application that is part of the suite of Google Docs Editors. It is comparable to Microsoft Excel, but unlike Microsoft Excel, it is hosted online and accessible from anywhere with an internet connection. Google Sheets enables users to create, edit, and collaborate in real time on spreadsheets. In addition, it provides several tools for formatting, analyzing, and sharing data. Here are some of Google Sheets' main features:

- Real-time interaction: Multiple users can work concurrently on the same spreadsheet, and everyone is automatically updated when modifications are made.
- Formulas and functions: Google Sheets offers a broad range of formulas and functions for performing calculations on data.
- Google Sheets can generate charts and diagrams to visually represent data.
- Filtering and sorting data: Google Sheets enables users to filter and classify data to locate the required information.
- Google Sheets can be used to validate data to ensure that it has been accurately entered.
- Google Sheets enables users to share spreadsheets with others and export them to a variety of formats, including PDF, Excel, and CSV.

Google Sheets is a potent utility that can be utilized for numerous purposes, including:

- Administration of resources
- Monitoring purchases
- Developing finances
- Analysis of data
- Presentation preparation
- Working in concert with others

Google Sheets is an excellent option for creating or editing spreadsheets. It is user-friendly, robust, and accessible from anywhere. Visit docs.google.com/spreadsheets/ to try out Google Sheets.

5.6   Google Sheets – Learning the Basics

This section will cover the fundamentals of using Google Sheets and its features.

- Bring up Google Sheets. This can be accomplished by visiting google.com/spreadsheets or going to Google Drive at https://drive.google.com/ and selecting the new button. Select Google Sheets next.

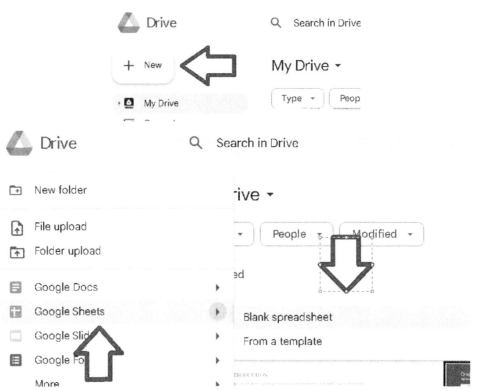

- Input your details. Clicking on cells and entering text to populate them is possible.
- Structure your data. You can modify the data's font, size, and color, as well as its alignment and borders.

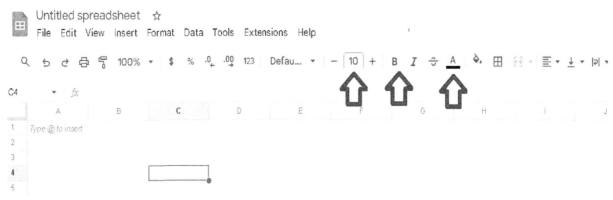

- Utilize equations and functions. You can use a variety of formulas and Functions to conduct calculations on your data in Google Sheets. The SUM() function, for instance, can be used to sum the values in a range of cells.

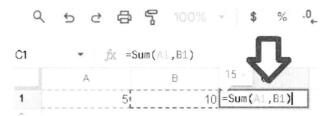

- Create graphs and infographics. Google Sheets can be used to generate charts and graphs for data visualization. For instance, the LINE() function can be used to create a line chart.

- Share your spreadsheet with others. You can allow others to access your spreadsheet by selecting the Share button.
- It would be best if you exported your spreadsheet. Your spreadsheet can be exported to a variety of formats, including PDF, Excel, and CSV.

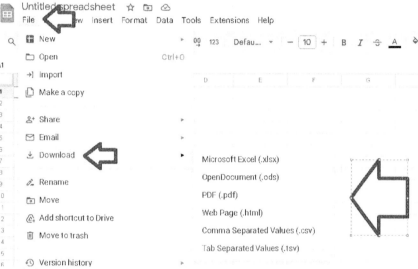

Here are some additional Google Sheets usage tips:

- Utilize keyboard shortcuts to maximize efficiency. Ctrl+Enter, for instance, can insert a new row beneath the existing one.
- Utilize the available templates to get started swiftly. Numerous templates are available for various purposes, including expense monitoring, budgeting, and task management.
- Utilize the conversation and comments functions to collaborate with others. You can use these features to add notes and pose questions about your spreadsheet.
- Utilize the filters and categorizing functions to locate the required information. These features can be used to locate specific data in your spreadsheet quickly.
- Use the data validation function to ensure that the entered data is accurate. This function prevents users from inputting invalid data into a spreadsheet.

5.7 Google Sheets - Data Management

Google Sheets is a powerful data management application. It provides various tools for organizing, sorting, filtering, and analyzing data. Here are some of Google Sheets' available data management features:

- By using data validation, you can ensure that all data entered your spreadsheet is valid. You can specify, for instance, that only numbers are allowed in a particular cell. Utilize data validation to ensure the validity of your data. This can aid in preventing spreadsheet errors.
- Apply uniform formatting to your data. This will improve the appearance of your spreadsheet and make it easier to comprehend.

- You can have cells highlighted based on their values using conditional formatting. For instance, you can highlight cells that exceed a certain value or contain text that matches a particular pattern. Utilize conditional formatting to emphasize essential data. This can expedite the identification of trends and patterns in your data.
- Formulas and functions: Google Sheets provides a variety of formulas and functions that you can use to perform calculations on your data. The SUM() function, for instance, can sum the values in a range of cells.
- Charts and graphs: You can visualize your data using charts and graphs. This can assist you in better comprehending the relationships between your data points. Utilize graphs and infographics to display your data. This can assist you in better comprehending the relationships between your data points.
- Using data filters, you can rapidly locate the information you need in your spreadsheet. For instance, you can filter your spreadsheet to only display entries containing a particular value. Utilize data filters to locate the information you require rapidly. This can help you save time and concentrate on the most essential data.
- Use descriptive identifiers for your columns and rows when managing data in Google Sheets. This will make it simpler to comprehend your data and locate the required information.
- Utilize annotations to annotate your data. This can assist in elucidating your data or provide additional information.
- Sorting: You can categorize your spreadsheet based on the column values. This can help you organize your data and make it easier to locate specific information.
- Importing and exporting data: You can import data from other sources into Google Sheets and export your data to PDF, Excel, and CSV, among others. This can help you consolidate and manage your data more efficiently.

These are some of the available data management features in Google Sheets. Using these features, you can manage your data efficiently and maximize your use of Google Sheets.

5.8 Google Sheet – Formulas and Functions

Google Sheets functions and formulas are powerful instruments that can be used to accomplish various tasks. Formulas are expressions that you enter to instruct Google Sheets on calculating a cell's value, whereas functions are predefined formulas that Google Sheets has created for you. To use a function in Google Sheets, enter the equal sign (=) in a cell, followed by the function's name and parameters. Arguments are the required values for a function to execute its calculation. The SUM function, for instance, accepts a range of cells as its operand and returns the sum of the values in that range.

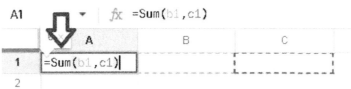

To use a formula in Google Sheets, input the formula expression followed by the equal sign (=). Formula expressions may contain references to cells, operators, and additional functions. The following formula, for instance, calculates the average of the values in cells C1 and D1:

Formula for calculating the average: =(C1+D1)/2

Google Sheets has a lot of formulas and functions, and not all may be used by the user. Here are some common and most used formulas and functions.

- The SUM function sums the values contained within a range of cells. For instance, the SUM(A1:A10) formula would add together the contents of elements A1 through A10.

- The AVERAGE function computes the meaning of a range of data. For example, the AVERAGE(A1:A10) formula would average the values of elements A1 through A10.
- The MAX function returns the greatest value within a given set of cell coordinates. For instance, the MAX(A1:A10) formula returns the highest value in the range of cells A1:A10.
- The MIN function returns the minimum value in a range of specified cells. MIN(A1:A10), for instance, returns the minimal value in the range of cells A1:A10.
- The COUNT function counts the number of elements in a range that contain numbers. For instance, the formula COUNT(A1:A10) would total the number of cells in the range A1 to A10 that contain numbers.
- The IF function permits decision-making based on the value of a cell. For example, the formula IF(A1>10, "Over 10", "Under 10") returns "Over 10" if the value in cell A1 is greater than 10 and "Under 10" otherwise.

5.9 Types of Function

Array Functions: A function in Google Sheets can return multiple values simultaneously. Calculations on various rows or columns of data are typically performed using array functions.

To utilize an array function in Google Sheets, enter the function into a cell and select Ctrl+Shift+Enter (or Cmd+Shift+Enter on a Mac). This instructs Google Sheets to consider the function an array function. Here are some examples of Google Sheets array functions:

- The SUMPRODUCT function multiplies the corresponding values and returns the sum of the values of the arrays ranging by two or more.
- The FILTER function returns a filtered variant of an array based on a condition that is specified.
- The UNIQUE function returns an enumeration of the array's unique values.
- ARRAY FORMULA: The ARRAY FORMULA function permits using functions that are not arrays with arrays.

Google Sheets array functions can be used for a variety of purposes. For instance, you can use the SUMPRODUCT function to determine the total sales for each product or the weighted average of a set of values. You can filter a list of data based on a condition or extract a subset of data from an array by using the FILTER function. By using the UNIQUE function, you can remove duplicate values from a list or generate a unique list of values from multiple arrays. Here is an example of using a Google Sheets array function:

Using a function, you can calculate the total sales for each product.

=SUMPRODUCT(A2:A10,B2:B10)

Where cells A2 to A10 contain the number of units sold and cells B2 to B10 contain the unit price.

Using a function, you can filter a list of data based on a specified condition.

=FILTER(C2:C10,D2:D10 = 100)

Cells C2 through C10 contain the data list, and D2 through D10 contain the condition.

Google Sheets array functions can be a powerful instrument for complex calculations. You can learn how to use array functions to save time and effort while creating more effective and informative spreadsheets with some practice.

Database Functions: A type of function that can be used to conduct calculations on data that is stored in a database. Data can be filtered, sorted, and aggregated using database functions, as well as other complex calculations. To use a database function in Google Sheets, a database range must first be created. A database range is a range of cells containing the data on which calculations are to be performed. After creating a database range, you can perform calculations on the data using database functions.

Here are some examples of Google Sheets database functions:

- DCOUNT: The DCOUNT function counts the number of database nodes that satisfy a given criterion.
- The DSUM function totals the values in a database range that satisfy a given criterion.
- The DAVERAGE function computes the average of the values in a database range that satisfy a given criterion.
- The DMIN function returns the minimum value in a database range that satisfies a given condition.
- DMAX: The DMAX function returns the largest value that satisfies a specified criterion within a database range.

Google Sheets database functions can be used for a variety of purposes. For instance, the DCOUNT function can be used to determine the number of consumers who have placed an order in each month. The DSUM function can be used to calculate the total sales for a specified product. You can calculate the average order value for a specified customer segment using the DAVERAGE function. The DMIN function can identify the consumer with the lowest order value. The DMAX function can identify the customer with the greatest order value. This demonstrates how to use a database function in Google Sheets:

The following formula could be used to calculate the total revenues for the month of April:

April = DSUM(A2:A10,B2:B2,"April")

A2 through A10 contain the order dates, while B2 through B10 contain the sales totals.

Database functions are an effective method for analyzing data recorded in a database. With some practice, you can learn to use database functions to save time and effort while creating more effective and informative spreadsheets.

Math Functions: A type of function that applies a mathematical operation to multiple cells. Math functions can be used to conduct basic elementary mathematical operations, including addition, subtraction, multiplication, and division, as well as more complex calculations, including trigonometric, statistical, and financial functions. These are some of the most frequently used math functions in Google Sheets:

- The SUM function totals a range of cells.
- The AVERAGE function computes the average of multiple columns.
- The MEDIAN function computes the median of a collection of cells.
- The COUNT function tallies the number of cells containing numbers in a range.
- The COUNTIF function calculates the number of cells in a range that satisfies a specified criterion.
- The SQRT function yields the square root of a given integer.
- The POWER function raises a given number to a specified power.
- The EXP function determines the exponential value of a given integer.
- The LOG function calculates the number's logarithm.
- The SIN function computes the sine of a given angle.
- The cosine of an angle is calculated by the COS function.
- The TAN function computes an angle's tangent.

In Google Sheets, math functions can be used to accomplish various duties. Using math functions, you can calculate, for instance, totals, averages, medians, and counts. Complex calculations, such as financial and statistical analyses, can also be performed using math functions.

Here is an example of how to use a Google Sheets math function:

To compute a month's total sales, you could enter the following formula in a cell:

=SUM(C2:C10)

Cells C2 through C10 contain the daily sales figures for the month.

Additionally, you can combine math functions with other functions. For instance, to compute the average order value for a customer, you could enter the formula =AVERAGE(SUM(E2:E10)) in a cell.

Cells E2 through E10 contain the order totals for each consumer order.

Google Sheets math functions are a potent instrument that can be used for various purposes. You can save time and create more informative spreadsheets by understanding math functions.

Date Function: A type of function that can be used to conduct calculations on dates and times. Date functions can be used to extract values such as the year, month, day, hour, minute, and second from a date and to conduct other complex calculations. Here are some examples of Google Sheets date functions:

- The DATE function returns a date value based on the year, month, and day specified.
- YEAR is a function that returns the year from a given date value.
- The MONTH function extracts the values of the month from a date value and returns it.
- The DAY function extracts the day from a date value and returns it.
- The HOUR function returns the hour from a given date and time.
- The MINUTE function returns the minute from a specified date and time.
- The SECOND function extracts the second from a date and time value and returns it.
- The DAYS function determines the number of days between two dates.

Google Sheets date functions can be used for a wide variety of purposes. Using the DATE function, for instance, you can construct a date value for a specific event, such as a birthday or anniversary. You can extract the year, month, and day from a date value using the YEAR, MONTH, and DAY functions. DAYS function. Using the DAYS function, you can calculate the number of days between two dates using a start date and an end date. Here is an example of how to use a Google Sheets date function:

To determine the number of days between a project's start and end dates, you could use the following formula:

=DAYS(A2,B2) Cell A2 contains the commencement date, and cell B2 contains the end date.

Google Sheets date functions can be powerful for working with dates and times. You can learn to use date functions to save time and create more effective and informative spreadsheets with a little practice.

Engineering Functions: A type of function that can be used to conduct engineering-application-typical calculations. Engineering functions can be used to calculate the properties of materials, such as density, strength, and elasticity, as well as the performance of engineering systems, such as a machine's efficacy or the flow rate of a fluid. The following are examples of engineering functions in Google Sheets:

- The function DELTA yields the difference between two numbers.
- ERF: The ERF function yields the integral of the Gauss error function over a specified interval.

- The ERF.PRECISE yields a more accurate value of the Gauss error function than using the ERF function.
- The GESTEP function returns a step function, which is equal to one value for a certain range of values and another value for a different range of values.

In Google Sheets, engineering functions can be used to execute a variety of tasks. For instance, the DELTA function can be used to calculate the change in temperature over time. You can use the ERF function to calculate the likelihood that a specific event will occur. You can use the ERF.PRECISE function to more precisely calculate the probability of a certain event occurring. You can use the GESTEP function to represent the behavior of a system by creating a step function.

Here is an example of how to use a Google Sheets engineering function:
The following formula may be used to calculate the change in temperature over time.

=Delta(C1,D1)

The beginning temperature is recorded in cell C1, and the ending temperature is recorded in cell B1.

For engineers and scientists, engineering functions can be a powerful instrument. With a little bit of practice, you can learn to use engineering functions to save time and effort while creating more effective and informative spreadsheets.

Filter Functions: A type of function that filters a range of data based on one or more specified criteria. The FILTER function returns a new data range containing only the values that satisfy the specified criteria. The FILTER function requires two arguments: the data range to be filtered and the filter criteria. The criteria may consist of a single or multiple conditions. If the criterion is a singular condition, the FILTER function will return a new data range containing only the rows that have met the condition. If the criteria are multiple conditions, the FILTER function returns a new range of data containing only the records that satisfy all the conditions. There are multiple methods to filter data using the FILTER function. For example, you can use the FILTER function to filter data by date, by text, by number, or by a combination of factors. The FILTER function can also be used to filter data from multiple ranges. Here is an example of how to use Google Sheets' FILTER function:

=FILTER(B2:D10, B2:B10="Fruit")

This formula returns a new data range containing only the rows from the range B2:D10, where the value in column B is "Fruit."

Here is an example of using multiple criteria with the FILTER function:

=FILTER(A2:D10, "Fruit":A2:A10, AND C2:C10>10)

This formula returns a new range of data containing only the entries from the range A2:D10 where the value in column A equal's "Fruit" and the value in column C exceeds ten.

The FILTER function is a potent instrument for filtering data in various methods. With a little practice, you can learn to use the FILTER function to save time and create more effective and informative spreadsheets.

Financial Functions: A type of function that can be used to conduct calculations on financial data. Financial functions can be utilized to calculate the present value and future value of cash flows, the internal rate of return, and the net present value of investments, as well as other complex financial calculations.

Here are some examples of Google Sheets's financial functions:

- Present Value: The PV function computes the present value of a series of prospective cash flows.
- FV: The FV function determines the present value of a series of prospective cash flows.
- IRR: The IRR function estimates the internal rate of return.
- NPV: The NPV function calculates an investment's net present value.
- PMT: The PMT function computes a loan's monthly payment.

Google Sheets' financial functions can be used for a variety of duties. For instance, the PV function can be used to determine the present value of a retirement savings plan. Calculate the future value of a college savings plan with the FV function. The IRR function can be used to determine the profitability of an investment endeavor. The NPV function is used to determine the attractiveness of an investment opportunity. The PMT function can be used to compute the monthly mortgage payment.

Here is how to use a financial function in Google Sheets:

The following formula may be used to determine the present value of a retirement savings plan:

=PV(0.10, 10, 2000)

The discount rate is 0.10, the number of years is 10, and the annual deposit is $2,000.

Financial professionals and investors can utilize financial functions as a powerful instrument. You can learn to use financial functions to save time and effort and make more informed financial decisions with a little practice. Please note that Google Sheets' financial functions are for informational purposes only and should not be used to make financial decisions. Please use the tool responsibly and thoroughly research before making decisions based on your finances.

Text Function: A type of function that applies an operation to text-containing cells. Text functions can be used to manipulate text in numerous ways, including string concatenation, substring extraction, and text formatting. These are some of the most frequently used text functions in Google Sheets:

- CONCATENATE is a function that concatenates two or more text sequences.
- LEFT yields the leftmost characters of a text string.
- The RIGHT function returns the rightmost characters of a string of characters.
- The MID function returns a substring of a text string beginning at a given position and continuing for a given number of characters.
- The TRIM function strips a text string of preceding and trailing spaces.
- The UPPER function capitalizes all characters in a Cell that contains text.
- The LOWER function transforms all the characters in a string of text to lowercase.
- The REGEXEXTRACT function extracts a substring from a text string that matches a regular expression.

In Google Sheets, text functions can be used to conduct various tasks. Using text functions, you can, for instance, put together data from multiple cells into a single cell, extract data from a text string, and format text in a particular manner. Here is an example of how to use a Google Sheets text function:

You could input the following formula into a cell to combine the first and last names of customers into a single cell:

Cell C2 contains the customer's first name, and cell E2 contains the customer's last name:

=CONCATENATE(C2, ", "E2).

Google Sheets' text functions are a powerful tool that can perform a variety of duties. By understanding text functions, you can manipulate text in a variety of ways and produce more informative spreadsheets.

Info Functions: A type of function that returns information about a single cell or a range of cells. The INFO function can return the following data:

- Type of information stored in the cell, such as text, numbers, dates, or times.
- The format of the data contained in a cell, such as general, number, date, or time.
- Protection of the cell: Whether the cell is protected from altering.
- Whether or not the cell has a comment.
- Contains a hyperlink if the cell contains one.

The INFO function requires two arguments: the cell or range of cells about which information is desired and the category of information to retrieve. Here is an example of how to use Google Sheets' INFO function:

=INFO("cell type", C1)

This formula returns the type of information contained in cell C1.

Here is another illustration of how to use Google Sheets' INFO function:

=INFORMATION(D1:D10, "cell protection")

This formula returns an array of values indicating whether the cells within the range D1:D10 are editable. The INFO function can be a useful tool for troubleshooting problems with spreadsheets or for obtaining information about the data in a spreadsheet.

Logical Functions: A type of function that can be used to compare multiple values and return a value based on whether the comparison satisfies the function's conditions.

Logical functions are utilized to compare multiple values and return a specified value or Boolean value (TRUE or FALSE) based on whether the comparison satisfies the function's conditions. In addition to being input into cells like all other functions, logical functions are frequently combined with other functions to create complex formulations.

Here are some examples of Google Sheets's logical functions:

- \> symbol is used to check if the value in a cell is greater than another cell's value and return TRUE if the condition is satisfied; else, return FALSE.
- < symbol is to check if the value in a cell is less than another cell's value and return TRUE if the condition is satisfied, else return FALSE.
- \>= symbol is used to check if the value in a cell is greater than or equal to another cell's value and returns TRUE if the condition is satisfied; else, return FALSE.
- <= symbol is to check if the value in a cell value is less than or equal to another cell's value and return TRUE if the condition is satisfied, return FALSE.
- = symbol is used to check if the value in a cell is equal to another cell's value and return TRUE if the condition is satisfied, else return FALSE.
- symbol is used to check if the value in a cell is not equal to another cell's value and return TRUE if the condition is satisfied, else return FALSE.

Here is an example of how to use Google Sheets' Logical function:

=(D1>=E1)

This checks if D1 is greater than or equal to E1, and if it is true, it will return TRUE, and if not, it will return FALSE. You may have already encountered functions with incorporated logical conditions in other sections. Logical functions can be utilized in a variety of applications and categories of spreadsheets, including data validation and the cleaning of cluttered datasets.

Lookup Functions: A type of function that is used to retrieve information from rows and columns corresponding to specific values found elsewhere in the worksheet or a distinct worksheet. Lookup functions can be particularly useful when searching for values in worksheets containing an astronomical number of rows and columns. Here are some examples of Google Sheets's Lookup functions:

=LOOKUP('search_key','search_column','return_column').
- Search_key represents the item you are looking for.
- Search_column indicates the column in which you are seeking for the item.
- Return_column specifies the required data.

Statistical Functions: A type of function that applies statistical calculations to a range of cells. Statistical functions can be used to compute different kinds of statistics like the mean, median, mode, and standard deviation and more complex statistical calculations like t-tests, chi-squared tests, and correlation coefficients. These are some of the most frequently used statistical functions in Google Sheets:
- The AVERAGE function computes the average of multiple columns.
- The MEDIAN function computes the median of a collection of cells.
- MODE is a function that determines the mode of a spectrum of cells.
- The STDEV calculates the standard deviation base on the provided cells.
- The COUNTIF function calculates the number of cells in a range that satisfies a specified criterion.
- The T.TEST function performs a t-test on two data groups to determine whether there is a statistically significant difference between the two groups' means.
- The CHI2TEST function performs a chi-squared test on two data sets to determine if the observed and expected values differ statistically significantly.
- The CORREL function calculates the coefficient of correlation between two cell ranges.

In Google Sheets, statistical functions can be utilized for various purposes. Statistical functions can be used, for instance, to calculate the average monthly sales, the median salary for a group of employees, or the standard deviation of a set of test scores. Statistical functions can also be used to conduct more complex statistical analyses, such as assessing the efficacy of a marketing campaign or comparing the performance of two products. Here is an example of using a Google Sheets statistical function:
You could enter the following formula in a cell to calculate the standard deviation of a set of test scores:

=STDEV(C2:C10)

In cells C2 to C10, the test scores are stored.

Google Sheets' statistical functions are a potent instrument that can be used for various purposes. You can obtain valuable insights into your data and make more informed decisions by learning how to use statistical functions.

Web Functions: A type of function that permits the import of data from a website into a spreadsheet. Web functions can extract data from a web page's tables, lists, and other structured elements.
The most frequently used web function in Google Sheets is IMPORTXML. The IMPORTXML function requires two arguments: the web page's URL and the XPath query to extract the data.
Here is an example of how to utilize the IMPORTXML function in Google Spreadsheet:

=IMPORTXML("https://www.google.com/finance/quote/AAPL", "//span[@class='price']")

This formula returns the present Apple Inc. stock price.

Additionally, you can use the IMPORTXML function to extract data from web page tables and listings. For instance, the following formula will extract the identities of all S&P 500 companies:

=IMPORTXML("https://en.wikipedia.org/wiki/List_of_S&P_500_companies", "//table[@class='wikitable']/tbody/tr/td[2]/a")

This function is used to import the list of S&P 500 companies. Importing data from web pages into Google Sheets is facilitated by web functions. By understanding web functions, you can save time and effort while creating more informative spreadsheets. Here are additional examples of using web functions within Google Sheets:

- The latest news headlines are extracted from a news website.
- Obtain the current weather forecast for a particular location.
- Import the product catalog from a web-based retailer.
- Obtain the most up-to-date stock prices for a list of companies

Web functions can be utilized to incorporate data from numerous web pages. You can automate duties and generate more dynamic and informative spreadsheets by learning how to use web functions.

5.10 Google Slides

Google Slides is a web-based presentation program included in the suite of Google Docs Editors. It is a free and simple-to-use program that allows users to create, modify, and distribute presentations. Therefore, users can effortlessly import and export presentations between Google Slides and Microsoft PowerPoint. Google Slides provides numerous features that make it a potent presentation tool. Users can incorporate text, images, videos, charts, and other elements into their presentations. They can also modify the appearance of their presentations by selecting from various themes and fonts. Google Slides offers several collaborative features, including sharing presentations with others and monitoring changes. Being a cloud-based application is one of the primary benefits of Google Slides. This allows users to access their presentations from anywhere with an internet connection. They can also collaborate on presentations with others in real-time. This makes Google Slides an especially useful tool for students, businesses, and other organizations that regularly need to create and distribute presentations. Google Slides is a versatile and effective presentation tool that is user-friendly and available to everyone. It is an excellent option for students, enterprises, and individuals who regularly need to create and distribute presentations.

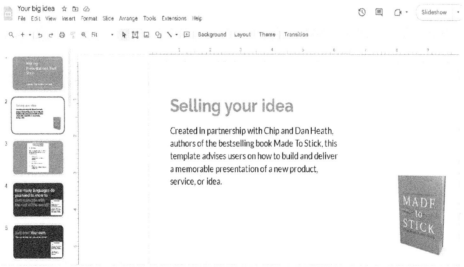

Among the features that make Google Slides a potent presentation tool are:

- Collaboration tools: Google Slides enables concurrent real-time work by numerous users on the same presentation. This facilitates team presentation collaboration and ensures everyone is on the same page.
- Google Slides provides extensive customization options, including themes, fonts, colors, and presentation layouts. This enables users to create presentations tailored to their needs and preferences.
- Google Slides enables users to incorporate multimedia elements into their presentations, including images, videos, and audio files. This facilitates the creation of visually enticing and engaging presentations.
- Google Slides offers an assortment of animation and transition effects to provide a robust visual appeal to presentations. This helps maintain audience interest and concentration during the presentation.
- Google Slides offers a presenter view that provides users with a live preview of their presentation and information about the current slide, forthcoming slides, and notes. This can assist users in delivering more assuring and captivating presentations.

In addition to these features, Google Slides offers a variety of additional beneficial features, including:

- Integration with other Google applications: Google Slides can work together with various Google apps, such as Google Docs, Google Sheets, and Google Drive. This makes creating and sharing presentations incorporating data from other Google applications simple.
- Offline editing: Google Slides enables users to edit their presentations when disconnected from the internet and then sync their modifications when they reconnect to the internet. This makes working on presentations simple even without an internet connection.
- Google Slides provides several accessibility features that make it simpler for individuals with disabilities to use the application. This includes text-to-speech, support for screen readers, and high contrast mode.

To try out Google Slides visit the link: slides.google.com

5.11 Creating Presentations

Follow these steps for creating a presentation using Google Slides:

- Open a web browser.
- Go to slides.google.com.

- You can click the "Blank" to create an empty presentation or choose a theme for your presentation.
- To add a title to your presentation, click "Click to add title."

- Click the + button in the upper left corner to add additional slides to your presentation.

Alternatively, you can add a new slide with a different layout by clicking the down arrow key beside the + button and selecting the desired layout.

- Customize the visuals and feel of your presentation by changing the theme, adding backgrounds, using transitions, and even making changes to the layout.

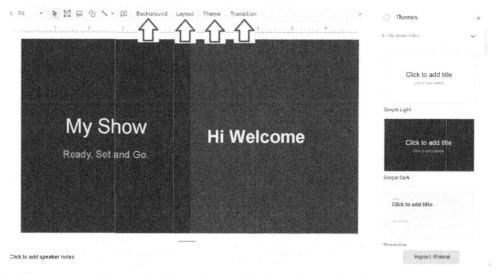

- Additionally, you can change the font, font style, font size, and color.

- To view a preview of your slide presentation, click the "Slideshow" button on the upper right.

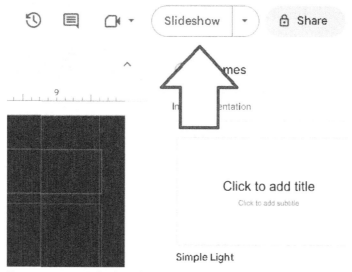

- You can adjust until you are satisfied with the presentation you have created. Congratulations, you now know the basics of making a slide presentation.

5.12 Collaboration Tips

First, we must learn how to share a presentation. Follow the procedure below:

- All you need to do to start sharing your presentation is to click on the "Share" button on the upper right beside the "Slideshow" button.

- Next you can either add people by using their email or you can change the "General access" to anyone with a link. Copy the link and give it to the person you wish to share. Then just click "Done" when you are finished.

- And you are done; you can now have people edit, comment, and work together on a single slide.

Google Slides makes it simple to collaborate with others on presentations. Here are some suggestions for maximizing Google Slides collaboration:

- Select the appropriate sharing permissions. When you share a presentation with others, you can grant them view-only, comment, or edit permissions. If you share the presentation with a large group of individuals, it is best to grant them view-only access so that they can view it but cannot make any changes. If you are sharing the presentation with a smaller group of individuals who will contribute, you can give them the ability to remark or edit the presentation. After clicking the "Share" button, click the settings button.

A new box will appear with the ability for you to decide on what is allowed.

Settings for "Testing"

- ✅ Editors can change permissions and share

- ✅ Viewers and commenters can see the option to download, print, and copy

- Utilize comments to communicate with your team. Without modifying the presentation, comments are a great way to communicate with your collaborators about the presentation. To comment, click the slide to which you wish to add the comment, and a text box appears for you to be able to type your comment. Your coworkers will be able to view and respond to your comments.

- Keep track of alterations. You can monitor presentation changes if you share your presentation with others who have edit access. Click the Review tab and then the Track Changes icon to monitor modifications. When you make alterations to the presentation, a new version will be generated, and your modifications will be tracked. You can examine the changes made to the presentation and either approve or refute the changes.

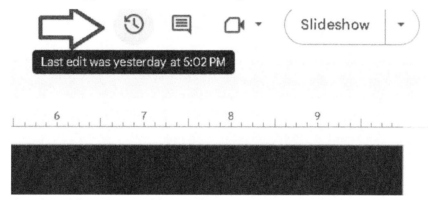

- Utilize a version log. The version history feature lets you view your presentation's previous iterations. This is useful if you need to revert to a previous version of the presentation or examine how a specific change was made. To view the version history, select "Version history" from the File menu.

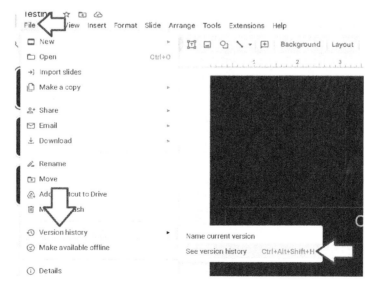

5.13 Google Forms

Google Forms is an online survey application included in the Google Workspace suite. It is a free and simple-to-use tool that enables users to construct and distribute surveys for data collection. Google Forms supports multiple question formats, including multiple-choice, checkbox, brief answer, long answer, and rating scale. In addition, users can submit images, videos, and other forms of multimedia to their surveys. After creating a survey, users can distribute it via email, social media, or a link. Respondents can then submit their responses online after completing the survey. Google Forms automatically accumulates and stores survey responses in a Google Sheet, where users can view, analyze, and share the data.

Google Forms is a versatile instrument that can be utilized for numerous purposes, including:
- obtaining feedback from clients or pupils
- carrying out market research
- evaluating employee contentment
- Collecting information for scientific research
- Creating tests and exercises

Google Forms is a potent instrument for collecting data from various individuals and organizations. It is user-friendly and provides a variety of features, making it a valuable instrument for data collection. To try out Google Forms visit the website forms.google.com.

5.14 Creating Forms

Follow these instructions to create a form with Google Forms:
- Google Forms can be accessed at https://forms.google.com/.
- Click the "Blank" to create your custom form or select one of the templates already available.

- Provide a title and description for your form.

- Include queries on the form. Multiple-choice, checkbox, brief response, extended response, and rating scale questions are available.

- Add multimedia elements such as images, videos, and audio to your form. You will need to click on the icons as shown below.

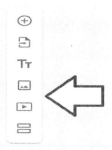

- Change the form's appearance by altering the theme, fonts, and colors. You must click the "Theme" icon on the upper right corner of the page. Once you do, a menu will appear for you to be able to adjust.

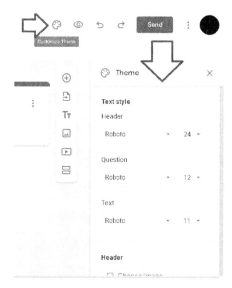

- To add more questions, click on the "Add question" icon.

- Same can be done for sections just click on "Add section: icon.

- When you have completed creating your form, you can send it to others by clicking the "Send" icon on the upper right corner of the page.

A new box will appear, and you can input the email addresses of the people you want. You may add a title or a short message, then click "Send" when you are done.

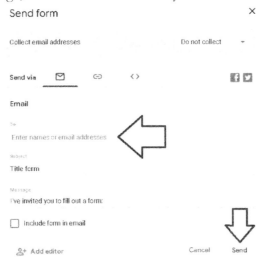

Another method is to copy or embed the link, where you can manually place it on a social media platform you wish people to see. But you can also directly share it on Facebook and Twitter. This is useful if you are trying to get responses from a large group of people or people you do not directly know.

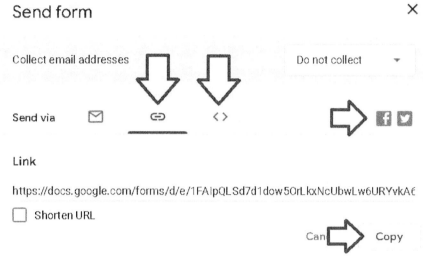

- With that you now know the basics of using Google Forms

5.15 Data Collection and Analysis

Google Forms facilitates data collection and analysis. After you have created and distributed a form, respondents can fill it out and submit their responses online. Google Forms collects and stores survey responses automatically in a Google Sheet. You may use the following features to observe and analyze the data in your Google Sheet:

- Summary tab: This page summarizes the responses to the survey, including the number of respondents, the number of responses for each question, and the most frequent responses.

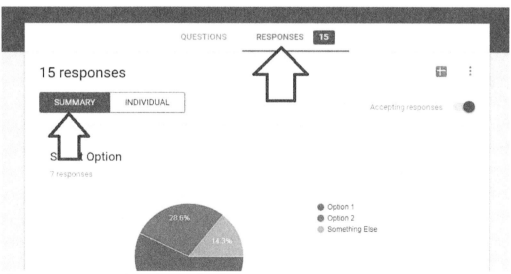

- Individual Responses tab: The Individual Responses tab displays all survey responses individually. This tab can be used to observe answers to specific questions or to identify data trends.

- Graphs and charts: You can visualize your data using a variety of chart and graph formats available in Google Sheets. This can enable you to identify trends and patterns in the data.
- Google Sheets can also be used to calculate statistics, including averages, percentages, and standard deviations. This can assist you in interpreting your data.

Once you have analyzed your data, you can export it to formats such as PDF, Excel, and CSV to share it with others. Click on the ⋮ icon to the right of the page and select "Download responses."

5.16 Google Translate

Google Translate is an online neural machine translation with multilingual capabilities as a free service that can translate text, documents, and websites between languages. It supports over 130 different languages from the Middle East, Asia, Europe, America, and more.

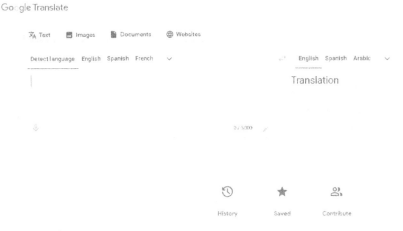

To translate text, Google Translate employs a neural network. Neural networks are an artificial intelligence system that can learn from data. Google Translate was trained in a massive corpus of text and code, enabling it to translate text accurately and fluently. Google Translate is a potent instrument that can be used for a variety of functions, including:

- Document translation for business or study
- Interacting with individuals of diverse linguistic backgrounds
- Web pages and articles in a foreign language
- Language acquisition

Google Translate is a fast and easy method to translate text between languages. It is accessible on a variety of devices, including computers, mobile phones, and tablets. It is also accessible to a global audience because it is available in multiple languages. To try out Google Translate visit the website translate.google.com.

5.17 How To Use Google Translate

Website

To translate text on the website of Google Translate:

- Visit translate.google.com to access the Google Translate website.
- Input the text you wish to translate into the field on the left.
- Choose the target language on the right box to which you want the left box to be translated.

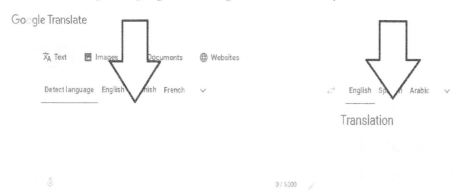

- The input text is instantaneously translated to the desired language and displayed on the right box.

- To change language, select the arrow symbol beside the other language choices.

- A box will appear showing a list of all the languages.

To translate images on the website of Google Translate:

- Visit translate.google.com to access the Google Translate website.
- Click on the Images tab.

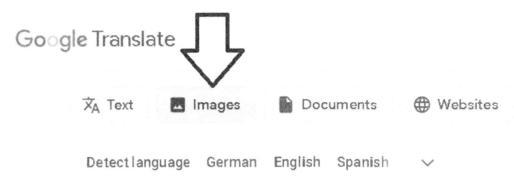

- Select the language representing the image on the left box, and on the right box, select the language you wish to translate into.

- Now either drag and drop an image into the specified field or choose one from your computer.

- Translation will be done automatically, and the result will show once done.

To translate documents on the website of Google Translate:

- Visit translate.google.com to access the Google Translate website,
- Click on the Documents tab.

- Select the language representing the document on the left box, and on the right box, select the language you wish to translate into.

- Now either drag and drop a document into the specified field or choose one from your computer.

- Click Translate to begin the translation.

- Click the Download translation to download the translated document.

To translate a website on the website of Google Translate:

- Visit translate.google.com to access the Google Translate website.
- Click on the Websites tab.

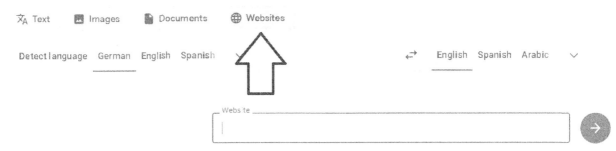

- Select the language representing the website on the left side, and on the right side, select the language you wish to translate into.

- Input the website URL link in the provided space and click the arrow.

- The website will pop up, and translations will have been applied.

Google Translate App

To translate text on the Google, Translate app:

- Download and install the Google Translate app from the Play Store.
- Open the Google Translate app.
- Type in the text on the box that you want to be translated.

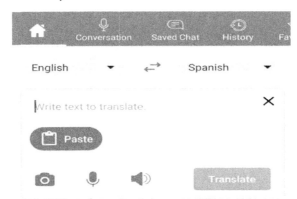

- You can change the language by clicking the arrow symbol on the right side of each language; remember that the right language is the language you will translate the input text into.

- A box will appear with all the available languages.

- Click the Translate button to begin translating the text.
- The translated text will appear on another box.

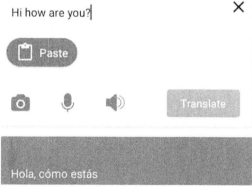

You can also use Google Translate to translate audio and video files. To translate your own audio:

- Open the Google Translate app
- Click on the ap the Mic button.

- Google Translate will now record your voice and speak clearly, and it should register.
- The words you have spoken will be registered and can now be translated.
- Select the appropriate language to be translated and click translate.

- A box below will pop up with the translation.

To translate an image file:
- Open the Google Translate app.
- Click on the camera icon

- You can take a picture using your camera or attach a saved image.

- Google Translate will translate the image; depending on how much text is in the picture, it will affect the time it takes for Google to translate them properly.
- Once done Google will display the translation

Google Translate is a potent instrument for translating text, audio, and video in over 100 languages. It is an excellent resource for anyone who needs to communicate with foreign-language speakers. Here are some additional Google Translate usage tips:
- You can compose in a variety of languages using the Google Translate keyboard.
- The Google Translate app allows for real-time text translation.
- Your preferred translations can be saved for future use.
- Your translations can be shared with others.

Google Translate is a complimentary service accessible to all users. It is a fantastic method to communicate with people from around the globe.

6 SCHEDULING & COLLABORATION

6.1 Google Calendar

Google Calendar is a prominent calendar service for time management and scheduling developed by Google. Users can create and modify events, set reminders, and share calendars. Google Calendar is a web application, mobile application, and desktop application. Google Calendar is a potent instrument that can be used to manage one's time and schedule effectively. Here are some of Google Calendar's most important features.

Create and modify occasions

Google Calendar facilitates the creation and modification of appointments. Each event can be given a title, description, location, start time, and end time. You can also include reminders, guests, and additional information. For instance, you can make an event for your team's upcoming meeting. You can include the meeting's title, description, location (for example, conference room A), start and end times. You can also provide the email addresses of your team members as meeting attendees so that they receive an invitation. Google Calendar enables you to set event reminders, which can be delivered via email, text message, or push notification. For instance, you can set a reminder 30 minutes before your next meeting to ensure you remember it. You can also set a reminder for the conclusion of your workday so that you know when it's time to leave for the day. Google Calendar enables you to share your calendars with other users. This is one of the best methods for staying organized and in sync with your team, family, and acquaintances. For instance, you can share your work calendar with your colleagues so they can see when you are available for meetings. Your calendar can be shared with your family and friends so they can view your activities. View your agenda in various formats: You can view your Google Calendar in a variety of methods, including by day, week, month, or year. You can also construct custom views to display the most important information to you. For instance, you can make a custom view to view all your upcoming events in one location. You can also construct a custom view for a specific project's events.

Integrate with Google's additional products

Google Calendar is compatible with other Google applications, including Gmail and Google Meet. This makes it simple to schedule meetings and events via email or a video conferencing app. To schedule a meeting directly from Gmail, select the "Schedule a meeting" button in the email compose window. Selecting the "Meet" button on the calendar allows you to schedule your meetings directly from Google Meet. Google Calendar is a potent and versatile utility that effectively manages your time and schedule. It is an excellent option for both personal and business use.

Here are some additional Google Calendar features that you may find useful:

- You can color-code your events to make them more easily discernible briefly. For instance, you can color-code work-related events in green, personal events in blue, and family events in red.

- Subcalendars: You can construct subcalendars to categorize your events. For instance, you can construct a subcalendar for your work events, one for your personal events, and one for your family events.

- You can establish objectives for yourself and monitor your progress over time. For instance, you can set a goal of running 60 minutes daily or reading one book monthly. Google Calendar will monitor and provide feedback on your progress.

- Google Calendar enables users to create and manage assignments. This makes it simple to keep track of your obligations.

Google Calendar is a dynamic application, with new features being introduced frequently. This makes staying organized easy and on top of your personal and professional schedule. To try out Google Calendar, visit the website calendar.google.com or download the Google Calendar app on your mobile devices.

6.2 The Ins and Outs of Google Calendar

Visit the Google Calendar website at calendar.google.com or download the Google Calendar app. Sign in with your existing Google account to use Google Calendar, or if you do not have one, create a Google account. Once logged in, the current day of your calendar will be displayed.

Creating A New Event

To create a new event, select "Create" and enter its details; include as much information as possible when creating a new event, including the title, description, location, start time, end time, and attendees. You may include additional information, such as a recurrence pattern, video conferencing link, or file attachment.

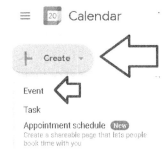

To modify an existing appointment, click on the event in your calendar. A popup box will appear, and you can edit or delete the event.

Customize Your View

Viewing your agenda in various formats: There are numerous methods to view your calendar on Google Calendar, including day view, week view, month view, and year view. You can also construct custom views to display the most important information to you. For instance, you could construct a custom view to see all your upcoming events in one location or to view all your events for a particular project.

To change the view of your calendar, go to settings, and under the General tab, pick the View options and choose the desired view, such as day, week, month, or year.

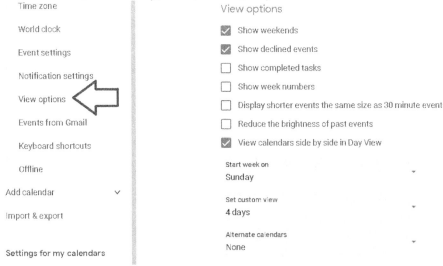

Share Your Calendar

To share your calendar, select the "Share" button and provide the email addresses of people you wish to share the calendar with. You can also share your calendar publicly or with only specific individuals. Consider establishing a shared, editable calendar if you share your calendar with coworkers. Developing a method like this is highly efficient in keeping everyone on the same page and preventing scheduling conflicts. Also, sharing may not be available on the Google Calendar app so you may need computer access. On the left area, look for the My calendars section and click on the three dots beside the calendar name.

Select the Settings and sharing and you will be taken to the settings for my calendar section.

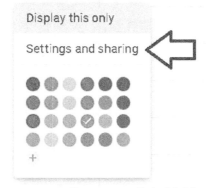

Under "Share with specific people or groups," you can click "Add people and groups."

A new box will appear, which allows you to share your calendar by adding people via email address or name. Then click send.

The recipient must select the link in the email to add the calendar to their list.

Integration of Google Calendar to other apps.

Integrating Google's other products: Google Calendar is compatible with other Google applications, including Gmail and Google Meet. This makes it simple to schedule meetings and events via email or a video conferencing app. To schedule a meeting directly from Gmail, select the "Schedule a meeting" button in the email compose window. To integrate Google Calendar with other Google products, such as Gmail and Google Meet, click on "Settings," then select your calendar, then under your calendar, click on the "integrate calendar" option.

Under the "integrate calendar" tab, look for the "Secret address" section and copy the link by clicking the copy link icon.

Use this address to access this calendar from other applications.

Warning: The address won't work unless this calendar is public.

Secret address in iCal format

••••••••••

You must now paste the copied link onto the other Google application.

Setting up Alerts and Notification

To set up alerts, go to "Settings," click on your calendar and go to the "Calendar settings" tab.

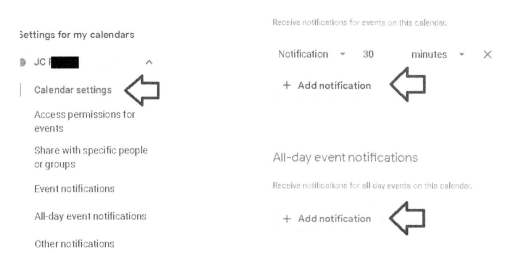

On the right side, under the "Event notifications" tab, you can make changes, delete, or add new notifications. You can also decide how long you wish to be reminded before the event and how you wish to be notified (email or text).

6.3   Google Meet

Google Meet is a video conferencing platform created by Google. It is a potent and flexible instrument that can be used easily for a variety of purposes, including:

- Hold video conferences with family, acquaintances, and coworkers. With just a few keystrokes, Google Meet makes it simple to connect with people around the world.

- Host online workshops and seminars. Google Meet can teach students and coworkers new skills and information.
- Perform employment interviews. Google Meet can be used to conduct job candidate interviews.
- Conduct presentations. Google Meet can be used to live-answer queries and share presentations with others.
- Collaborate on project development. Google Meet can be used to collaborate remotely on initiatives with others.

Google Meet provides several features that make it an excellent option for video conferencing, such as:
- Google Meet provides high-quality video and audio through cutting-edge technology, even in low-bandwidth conditions.
- Google Meet permits you to share your screen with other participants to collaborate on documents, presentations, and other projects.
- Google Meet provides real-time captions so that everyone can partake in a meeting regardless of hearing ability.
- Google Meet employs noise cancellation to reduce background noise, allowing you to concentrate on the meeting without being distracted.
- Breakout rooms: Google Meet enables the creation of breakout rooms for smaller, more focused discussions.
- Google Meet can monitor meeting attendance so that you can see who attended.
- Google Meet integrates with other Google products, such as Gmail and Google Calendar, allowing you to schedule and join meetings easily.

Google Meet is offered as a web application, a mobile application, and a desktop application. It is free for personal accounts and offers paid plans with additional features, such as extended meeting times and larger meeting capacities, for businesses and organizations. Here are some additional Google Meet usage tips:
- Use a headset or microphone of high quality to enhance the sound quality of your calls.
- Make sure you have a stable internet connection to prevent video and audio delays.
- Utilize a virtual background to obscure or replace your background with an image or video.
- Mute your microphone when you're not speaking to prevent extraneous noise.
- Use the chat function for sending messages to other call participants.
- You should record your meetings to view them later or to share with others.

Google Meet is an excellent tool for remote communication and project collaboration. Here are a few guidelines that will help you maximize Google Meet and conduct productive and pleasant video calls. Here are a few examples of how Google Meet can be utilized in various contexts:
- Educators can utilize Google Meet to teach online classes, conduct office hours with students, and collaborate with other educators.
- Businesses can use Google Meet for video meetings with employees, clients, and partners, employment interviews, and webinars.
- Google Meet can be used by nonprofits to host board meetings, volunteer training sessions, and fundraising events.
- Personal: Google Meet can be used to remain in touch with far-flung friends and family, to celebrate special occasions, and to play online games.
- Google Meet is an excellent tool for remaining connected and collaborating with others, regardless of your needs.

To try out Google Meet, visit the website meet.google.com or download the Google Meet app on your mobile devices.

6.4   Learning How to Meet

How to Host a Meeting

Be on the Google Meet website or have the Google Meet app opened and sign into your Google account.
You can host in Google Meet by following these steps:
Visit the Google Meet website or launch the Google Meet app on your device.

Sign in with your Google account if you still need to access your Google account.
Click the "New meeting" button to initiate a meeting.

Choose whether you wish to have an immediate meeting or schedule one for a later date.

⊂⊃   **Create a meeting for later**

\+   **Start an instant meeting**

☐   **Schedule in Google Calendar**

On the next screen, you must choose between "allow microphone and camera," which is recommended
to experience Google Meet properly, or "Continue without microphone and camera."

If done correctly, your meeting room should be up now. You need to add people to the meeting room.
Usually, when you start a meeting, a box will pop up at the lower left side, prompting you to add people
using their name or email or copy the link and provide it to them.

If the pop-up box did not appear, then you will need to look for the "show everyone" icon on the lower right of the screen and click it.

A new box will appear on the right side of the screen. To add people, click the "Add people" icon or search for the name or email of a specific person in the space provided.

Once inside the meeting, it is possible to see and hear the other participants. In addition, you can share your screen, record the meeting, and mute yourself.

Joining a Meeting

Joining a meeting is a much simpler task. You first need to be at the Google Meet website or open the Google Meet app while logging in to your Google Account. Look for the join section on the website or app, and you should be able to input the join code or link to access the meeting.

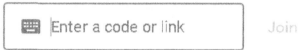

6.5   Google Meet Additional Features

Screen Sharing

You must first be in a meeting to allow screen sharing in Google Meet. When you are in a meeting, look at the lower icons and click on the "Present now" icon.

A new box will appear, allowing you to select what you want to share and click the "Share" button.

Adding a Virtual Background

You must first be in a meeting to apply a virtual background in Google Meet. When you are in a meeting, look at the lower icons and click on the three-dot icon.

A box will appear, and now select "Apply visual effects."

A box will appear to your right; you can select between an assortment of backgrounds here. Click on the one you desire, and it will automatically change your background.

Turning Captions on or Off

You must first be in a meeting to turn captions on or off in Google Meet. When you are in a meeting, look at the lower icons and click on the "Caption" icon.

If the caption is not on, clicking it will set it to on, and if you are to click it again, it will turn off. When it is on, you will see a box below your video; when you talk, it will register what you have said in text.

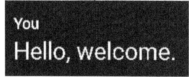

Recording Videos and Live Streaming

You must first be in a meeting to record videos or live stream in Google Meet. When you are in a meeting, look at the lower right icons and click on the "Activities" icon.

A box will appear on the right side of the screen. Select whether you want to live stream by clicking "Live streaming" or "Recording" to record a video.

6.6 Google Jamboard

Google Jamboard is a digital whiteboard that enables real-time collaboration. It is an excellent instrument for creativity, presentation, and brainstorming. Jamboard provides numerous features, including:

- You can add sticky notes to your Jamboard to communicate your thoughts and ideas. Sticky notes can also be moved, resized, and color-coded.
- Freehand drawing: Using the freehand drawing instrument, you can draw on your Jamboard. You have the capability to add text, images, and shapes.
- Collaboration: You can share your Jamboard with others and collaborate with them in real-time. You can view the drawings and programming of others in real time.
- You can present your Jamboard by sharing your screen with others or projecting it onto a large screen.

Jamboard is a website, a mobile application, and a hardware device. The web application and mobile application are complimentary for all users. Google makes the hardware device available for purchase. Here are some examples of uses for Google Jamboard:

- Jamboard is an excellent instrument for brainstorming new ideas. You can easily communicate your ideas and thoughts with post-it notes and illustrations. You can also collaborate with others in real time to generate new concepts.
- Jamboard can also generate ideas for new products, services, or features. Create wireframes, mockups, and prototypes using post-it notes and hand-drawn sketches. You can also refine your concepts through real-time collaboration with others.
- Jamboard can also be used to communicate your concepts to others. You can project your Jamboard onto a wall or display it on a large screen. Presentation mode can also be used to accentuate specific elements of your Jamboard.
- Jamboard can be used in the classroom to facilitate pupil learning and collaboration. Teachers can use Jamboard to present lessons, facilitate discussions, and assign homework. Using Jamboard, students can take notes, create presentations, and collaborate on projects.
- Jamboard can be used in business to facilitate employee collaboration and problem-solving. Utilizing Jamboard, companies can hold ideation sessions, develop new products and services, and give client presentations.

Google Jamboard is a potent and flexible instrument that can be utilized for various purposes. It is an excellent tool for creativity, presentation, and collaboration. Here are some additional Google Jamboard usage tips:

- Use distinct colors for various content types. For instance, yellow sticky notes could be used for ideas, green sticky notes for inquiries, and red sticky notes for action items.
- Utilize images and videos to enhance the visual allure and engagement of your Jamboards.
- Use the presentation mode to highlight your Jamboard's specific elements and deliver a more polished presentation.
- Save your Jamboards to Google Drive to access them from any location.
- Share your Jamboards with others so they can view your presentation or collaborate with you.

Google Jamboard is an excellent instrument for collaboration, creativity, presentation, and brainstorming. By following these guidelines, you can maximize Google Jamboard and accomplish more. To try out Google Jamboard, visit the website jamboard.google.com or download the Google Jamboard app on your mobile devices.

6.7   Basics of Google Jamboard

Creating a New Jam

Head onto the Google Jamboard website. Select the "New Jam" icon on the lower right.

If done correctly, you will now have a new Jam opened.

On the top, you can change the background by selecting "Set background" or "Clear frame" to wipe the board clean.

The icons to the left contain the following: a pen tool for drawing, an eraser tool to remove segments, a selection tool, sticky notes, images, shapes, a text box, and a laser pointer.

Google Jamboard is a free-range tool; the only limit will be your imagination.

6.8   Google Keep

Google Keep is an app developed by Google for notetaking. It is offered as a web, mobile, and desktop application. You can create and organize notes, lists, and images with Google Keep. Additionally, you can add labels and hues to make your notes easier to locate. Google Keep also offers a variety of collaborative features, such as the capability to share notes and create to-do lists.

Here are some of Google Keep's applications:

- Google Keep is an excellent instrument for taking notes in class, at work, or while traveling. Creating text notes, image notes, and audio notes is possible. You can also include sketches and illustrations in your notes.
- Google Keep can help you manage your thoughts and ideas by organizing them. You can create nested notes, add labels and colors to your notes, and generate lists.

- Google Keep enables you to share and collaborate in real-time on notes with others. Additionally, you can create to-do lists and delegate tasks to others.
- Google Keep can help you to remember things by creating reminders and notifications. You can set yourself or others as a reminder. Additionally, you can receive alerts when someone shares a note with you or when a task is due.

Google Keep is a potent and flexible application that can be used for various purposes. It is an excellent instrument for taking notes, organizing ideas, collaborating with others, and remembering information. Here are some additional Google Keep usage tips:

- Use distinct hues for distinct categories of notes. For instance, blue notes could be used for work, green for school, and red for personal notes.
- Label your notes to organize them into categories. You could establish labels for various projects, classes, or topics.
- Utilize the search bar to swiftly and easily locate notes.
- Utilize the archive feature to conceal notes you do not need to view frequently.
- Use the share feature to collaborate on initiatives or to share notes with others.

Google Keep is an excellent organization and productivity tool. By following these guidelines, you can maximize Google Keep and accomplish more. To try out Google Keep, visit the website keep.google.com or download the Google Keep app on your mobile devices.

6.9   How to Use Google Keep

First, open the Google Keep website or Google Keep app to use Google Keep.

You can start taking notes on the webpage by clicking on the "Take on note" icon. You can also provide a title if you desire to.

The icons below the note allow you to on notifications, add images, share, change background color, and even archive it for later use.

Click "Close" when you are done typing and modifying your note. Your note will be stuck onto the page like a sticky note when you write down your note.

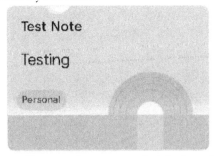

On the left part of the screen, you will see a few premade labels, which is where your notes are being stored. The notes are kept on the label you are working on, except the "Note" label, which shows all notes from all labels, and the "Reminder" label is where you can see all notes with notifications.

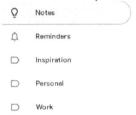

Below the labels, you will have additional icons like "Edit label," which allows you to edit the pre-existing labels or create new labels; the "Archive" icon, where you can view all the notes you have archived; and "Trash" icon, where you can view discarded notes which you can restore or delete forever.

Google Keeps is an easy and efficient tool for people who love notetaking.

7   NAVIGATION & REAL-WORLD TOOLS

7.1   Google Maps

Google Maps is a web-based mapping application created by Google. With over 1 billion active users, it is one of the most widely used mapping services globally. Google Maps provides numerous characteristics, including:

- Google Maps offers high-definition satellite imagery of the entire planet. This can be helpful for investigating new locations, planning trips, and gaining a deeper understanding of the world around you.

- Google Maps also offers street maps for most cities and villages worldwide. These maps contain comprehensive information about highways, streets, and structures.

- Google Maps Street View provides 360-degree panoramic views of streets in numerous cities worldwide. You can gain a better understanding of a location's appearance prior to your visit.

- Google Maps provides real-time traffic conditions for most significant roads and highways. This information can assist you in avoiding traffic congestion and reaching your destination more quickly.

- Google Maps can provide turn-by-turn driving, walking, biking, and public transportation directions. This can be useful for navigating unfamiliar areas and trip planning.

- Listings for enterprises: Google Maps includes listings for businesses from around the globe. These listings include the address, phone number, website, and hours of operation for each establishment. Additionally, you can browse reviews of businesses left by other users.

- Google Maps includes information about restaurants, hotels, museums, and parks around the globe, as well as other points of interest. You can search for attractions by name, category, or location.

- Google Maps provides multiple travel modes, including normal, traffic, and satellite. You may select the driving mode that best meets your requirements.

- Google Maps indoor maps Indoor maps depict the interiors of numerous structures, including airports, shopping malls, and museums. This can be useful for navigating large structures and locating specific businesses and services.

- Google Maps Live View. Live View overlays real-time coordinates and information on the real world, allowing you to navigate unfamiliar areas or locate specific businesses and services.

Google Maps is a potent and flexible instrument that can be utilized for a variety of purposes. It is an excellent tool for navigating, planning trips, discovering new locations, and locating businesses and services. Here are some additional Google Maps operating tips:

- Utilize the search bar to swiftly and easily locate locations.

- Utilize the layers feature to view various data types, such as traffic conditions, public transportation routes, and satellite imagery, on the map.

- Use the directions function to obtain turn-by-turn driving, strolling, cycling, and public transportation directions.

- Utilize the save function to store locations you wish to visit later.

- Utilize the share function to share locations with others.

- Utilize Street View to obtain a 360-degree panoramic view of a location.

- Utilize the Indoor maps feature to navigate large buildings.

- Utilize Live View to obtain real-time directions and information superimposed on the actual environment.

Google Maps is an ever-changing service, with new features being introduced frequently. By following these guidelines, you can maximize Google Maps and accomplish more. To try out Google Maps, visit the website maps.google.com or download the Google Maps app on your mobile devices.

7.2   Google Lens

Google Lens is a search tool for detecting visuals or images that employs machine learning to recognize objects, translate text, and assist with shopping. It is available as a mobile app and a Google Search feature. Google Lens is useful for:

- Google Lens can identify various objects, including vegetation, animals, products, landmarks, and works of art. This is beneficial for discovering more about the world around you, locating information about specific objects, and resolving issues. For instance, you could use Google Lens to identify a plant in your backyard, obtain information about a product you're considering purchasing, or diagnose a problem with your vehicle.
- Google Lens can translate text from one language to another in real-time. This can help interpret signs and menus in a foreign country, translate documents, and communicate with native speakers. You could, for instance, use Google Lens to translate a sign in a Japanese restaurant, a document from English to Spanish, or a conversation with a Chinese-speaking individual.
- Google Lens can help you purchase by providing product information, including prices, reviews, and locations. Google Lens has the capability to identify barcodes and QR codes to obtain product information and make purchases. Using Google Lens, you could, for instance, compare the price of a product at various stores, read reviews, or purchase the product online.
- Google Lens can provide information about locations, including addresses, phone numbers, hours of operation, reviews, and photographs. Google Lens can also provide coordinates to locations. Using Google Lens, you could, for instance, discover the address of a restaurant, read reviews of a hotel, or obtain directions to a museum.
- Google Lens is a potent and flexible instrument that can be utilized for various purposes. It is an excellent resource for learning about the world, translating languages, purchasing, and researching locations.

Here are some additional Google Lens usage tips:

- Ensure the object or text you are attempting to identify is in sharp focus and well-illuminated.
- If you're translating text, ensure that the text is readable by Google Lens.
- If you're seeking information about a location, make sure the location is centered in the frame.
- Google Lens has the capability to search for images online. Touch the search icon in the lower-right corner of the display, and then touch the image you wish to search for.
- Google Lens is perpetually evolving, and new features are being added regularly. Check the Google Lens support center for the most recent updates and recommendations.

Here are a few examples of how Google Lens can be utilized in various contexts:

- Google Lens can be used in the classroom to help students learn about their surroundings and complete assignments. Using Google Lens, a pupil could, for instance, identify a plant in the schoolyard, translate a passage from a textbook in a foreign language, or obtain information about a historical landmark.

- Google Lens can be used by businesses to increase sales and enhance customer service. For instance, a business could use Google Lens to translate a customer's query into another language, provide product information, or assist a customer in locating a product in a store.
- Individuals can use Google Lens to learn new things, remain in touch with family and friends, and simplify daily tasks. A user could, for instance, use Google Lens to learn about a new recipe, translate a menu written in a foreign language, or obtain directions to a friend's home.

Google Lens is a versatile and useful instrument that people of all ages and professions can use for various purposes. To try out Google Lens, visit the website lens.google.com or download the Google Lens app on your mobile devices.

8 ADVANCED FEATURES

8.1 Google Workspace Marketplace

The Google Workspace Marketplace is an online store where users and administrators can search and install third-party applications that integrate with Google Workspace applications. These apps can extend the functionality of Google Workspace apps and integrate them with other products and services that users and organizations utilize for work, education, or play. Here are some uses for Google Workspace Marketplace applications:

- Apps such as Asana, Trello, and Monday.com can assist users in tracking tasks, managing deadlines, and collaborating on projects.
- Apps such as Dropbox Paper, DocuSign, and Lucidchart enable users to create, revise, and share documents collaboratively.
- Time and expense monitoring: Applications such as Harvest, Toggl, and Expensify can assist users with time and expense tracking.
- Apps such as Wix, Squarespace, and WordPress can assist users in the creation and administration of their own websites.
- Communication with consumers and colleagues is facilitated by applications such as Zoom, Slack, and Microsoft Teams.
- Education: Apps such as Khan Academy, Google Classroom, and Edmodo can assist instructors in developing and delivering lessons, monitoring student progress, and communicating with students and parents.
- Apps like Salesforce, HubSpot, and Zoho CRM can assist businesses in managing sales prospects, customer relationships, and marketing campaigns.

In addition to apps specifically designed for healthcare, retail, and finance, the Google Workspace Marketplace also features a variety of apps designed for other industries and professions, such as retail, hospitality, and finance.

Advantages of utilizing Google Workspace Marketplace:

- Access to a variety of applications: The Google Workspace Marketplace provides access to a variety of applications from a variety of developers. This means that, regardless of your industry or position, you can discover apps that meet your specific needs.
- Installing applications from the Google Workspace Marketplace is simple and straightforward. Click "Install" to automatically install the application.
- Google examines each app in the Google Workspace Marketplace for compliance and security. This means that you can install applications with confidence that they are safe and secure.
- Numerous applications in Google Workspace Marketplace are gratis to install and utilize. Paid apps typically provide a free trial so that you can evaluate them prior to purchase.

How to utilize the Google Workspace Market:

To access Google Workspace Marketplace, go to the website and peruse the available applications. You can search for applications based on category, keyword, or popularity. Once you have located the app you wish to install, select the "Install" button. Administrators can also deploy applications on behalf of their users. To accomplish this, navigate to the Marketplace section of the Google Admin console. You can then peruse the available apps and install them on your user's behalf. Google Workspace Marketplace is an excellent resource for extending the functionality of Google Workspace applications and making them more effective for your organization. Here are some additional Google Workspace Marketplace tips:

- Please peruse app reviews prior to installing them. This can help you identify prospective issues with the applications.
- Check the permissions requested by applications before installing them. Only install programs that require the permissions they request.
- Disable applications that you no longer use. This can enhance the functionality of your Google Workspace applications.
- Keep your applications updated. Regularly, app developers release updates that repair bugs and add new features.

Google Workspace Marketplace is a valuable resource for Google Workspace customers and administrators. By following these guidelines, you can maximize Google Workspace Marketplace and maximize your Google Workspace applications. To try out Google Maps, visit the website workspace.google.com/marketplace.

8.2 API's and Third-Party Integration

The Google Workspace API is a collection of APIs that allows developers the opportunity to create new applications that integrate with Google Workspace apps. This allows developers to create applications that extend the functionality of Google Workspace apps or connect them to other products and services. The process of connecting Google Workspace applications to other products and services is known as third-party integration. This can be accomplished via the Google Workspace API or other methods, including webhooks or Zapier. The following are examples of how the Google Workspace API can be used to develop third-party integrations:

- Using the Google Workspace API, a developer could construct an application that enables users to create and manage Google Docs from within another application, such as a project management tool.
- Using the Google Workspace API, a developer could construct an application that allows users to automatically send emails from Gmail when specific events occur in another application, such as a customer relationship management system.

- Using the Google Workspace API, a developer could build an application that enables users to synchronize their Google Calendar events with their calendar in another application, such as an enterprise resource planning (ERP) system.

Advantages of using third-party Google Workspace integrations:

- Increased productivity: Third-party integrations can help users be more productive by automating tasks and connecting Google Workspace apps to the other tools they use.
- Improved collaboration: Third-party integrations can help users collaborate more effectively with others by facilitating information sharing and collaborative project work.
- Increased flexibility: Third-party integrations enable users to tailor Google Workspace apps to their specific requirements, thereby increasing their flexibility.
- Cost savings: Third-party integrations can help businesses save money by removing the need to acquire and maintain multiple software applications.\

Examples of third-party Google Workspace integrations:

- Zapier is a web-based automation application that enables users to connect various products and services. Zapier integrates with Google Workspace, allowing users to construct zaps that automate tasks between Google Workspace applications and other products and services.
- Asana is an application for project management that allows users to monitor tasks, manage deadlines, and collaborate on projects. Asana is integrated with Google Workspace, allowing users to create tasks in Asana from Gmail and view Asana tasks in Google Calendar.
- Salesforce is a customer relationship management application (CRM) that enables companies to manage sales prospects, customer relationships, and marketing campaigns. Salesforce is integrated with Google Workspace, allowing users to generate sales leads from Gmail and view Salesforce leads in Google Calendar.

Google Workspace API and third-party integrations can be an excellent method to use for the extension of the functionality of Google Workspace apps, boosting productivity and reducing costs.

8.3   Automation and Workflow Management

Google Workspace automation and workflow management is the use of Google Workspace applications and tools to automate tasks and optimize processes. This can help businesses increase efficiency, decrease expenses, and boost employee satisfaction. Google Workspace offers a variety of options for automating and managing workflows, including:

- Google Apps Script is an application that enables the creation of custom scripts to automate operations in Google Workspace applications. For instance, you could use Google Apps Script to create a script that automatically sends emails to customers when they place an order or creates a new project in Asana when a new lead is created in Salesforce.
- Google Forms and Sheets: By connecting Google Forms and Sheets to other Google Workspace applications or third-party services, it is possible to construct automated workflows. For instance, you could use Google Forms to create a form for customers to submit orders and then use Google Sheets to create a new order in your CRM system automatically.
- Google Workspace integrates with a variety of third-party services, including Zapier, Asana, and Salesforce. These integrations enable the automation of procedures between Google Workspace applications and other products and services. For instance, you could use Zapier to construct a zap that creates a new task in Todoist whenever a new email arrives in Gmail.

Here are some examples of how various industries can implement Google Workspace automation and workflow management:

- Order processing, customer service, and inventory management can be automated using Google Workspace automation and workflow management. For instance, a retail business could use

Google Apps Script to create a script that automatically sends a confirmation email to a customer when they place an order or to create a script that generates an inventory report at the end of each day.

- Automation and workflow management in Google Workspace can automate manufacturing tasks such as production planning, quality control, and supply chain management. A manufacturing company, for instance, could use Google Sheets to create a production schedule. Then, Google Apps Script creates a script that automatically notifies employees when duties are due.

- Google Workspace automation and workflow management can be used to automate healthcare duties, including patient scheduling, medical records management, and billing. A healthcare provider could use Google Forms to create a form that patients can use to schedule appointments and then use Google Apps Script to create a script that automatically adds the appointments to the provider's calendar.

- Education: Google Workspace automation and workflow management can be used to automate assignment grading, student progress monitoring, and parent communication. A teacher could, for instance, use Google Apps Script to construct a script that automatically grades assignments and sends feedback to students or to send weekly progress reports to parents.

Overall, Google Workspace automation and workflow management can be a fantastic method for businesses and organizations of all sizes to increase productivity, decrease expenses, and boost employee satisfaction. Here are some guidelines for implementing automation and workflow management in Google Workspace:

- Identify the duties and workflows that you wish to automate as a first step. What are the repetitive and time-consuming tasks? Which workflows could be made more efficient?

- Select the appropriate tools and platforms for your requirements. There are numerous Google Workspace apps and tools that can be used to automate duties and workflows, in addition to several third-party integrations. Consider your unique requirements and demands when selecting tools and platforms.

- Gain the support of your team members. Before implementing any adjustments to your workflows, it is necessary to obtain the support of your team members. Explain that automation is an advantage and how it will facilitate their work.

- Start small and progressively expand. It is preferable to start small and increase automation efforts incrementally. This will assist you in avoiding potential issues and ensuring that your automation is functioning as intended.

- Monitor your progress and make necessary adjustments. After implementing automation, monitoring its progress, and making necessary adjustments is essential. This will assist you in ensuring that your automation functions as effectively as feasible.

Automation and workflow management in Google Workspace can be a potent instrument for enhancing the efficiency and productivity of your business or organization. By following these guidelines, you can optimize Google Workspace automation and workflow management.

8.4 Mobile Management and Features

Google Workspace mobile management is a collection of features that enables businesses to manage their employees' mobile devices. This includes enrollment of devices, app management, security policies, remote resets, and more. Google Workspace mobile management supports Android, iOS, and Windows devices. Additionally, it is compatible with numerous mobile device management (MDM) solutions, such as MobileIron, VMware AirWatch, and Citrix Endpoint Management. Here are some additional details about Google Workspace's mobile management features:

- Organizations may mandate that employees enroll their mobile devices with Google Workspace mobile management. This provides the organization with complete control over the device's data. User enrollment and admin enrollment are the two categories of device enrollment. The most prevalent form of enrollment, user enrollment, enables employees to enroll their own devices in Google Workspace mobile management. Typically used for corporate-owned devices, Admin enrollment enables administrators to enroll devices on behalf of employees.

- Organizations can deploy and manage applications on the mobile devices of their employees. This includes applications from the Google Play Store, Apple's App Store, and other app stores. Organizations can also develop their own applications and deploy them to their employees' mobile devices.

- Organizations can implement security policies for the mobile devices of their employees. This includes password requirements, device encryption, remote erasure, and other policies. An organization could, for instance, require employees to use strong passwords, encrypt their devices, and enable administrators to erase data from lost or stolen devices remotely.

- Organizations can remotely delete data from the mobile devices of their employees. This can be beneficial if an employee decides to leave the company or when a device is lost or stolen. Remote wiping will erase all data, including personal information, from the device, so using this feature only as a last resort is essential.

Additional features of Google Workspace mobile management include:

- Conditional access allows the restriction of access by organizations to Google Workspace apps and data based on the condition of the device and user. An organization could, for instance, configure conditional access to prevent employees from accessing Google Workspace apps on devices not enrolled in Google Workspace mobile management.

- Endpoint detection and response (EDR) is a security solution that allows organizations to detect and respond to endpoint threats like mobile devices. EDR can assist businesses in detecting and removing malware, investigating security incidents, and responding to attacks.

- Zero-touch enrollment enables organizations to enroll corporate-owned Android devices in Google Workspace mobile management automatically. Zero-touch enrollment can aid companies in streamlining the device deployment procedure and spiraling IT staff.

Google Workspace mobile management is a potent instrument that can help businesses enhance their mobile device management's security, compliance, and cost-effectiveness. By utilizing Google Workspace mobile management, businesses can protect their data, ensure that their employees use secure devices, and reduce the likelihood of security breaches.

9   SECURITY & COMPLIANCE

Google Workspace Security and Compliance is a collection of features and services that assist businesses in protecting their data and adhering to industry regulations and standards. It offers extensive features, including data encryption, access controls, security auditing, and compliance tools. Google Workspace encrypts all stored and transmitted data. This ensures that data is secure, even if it is lost or stolen. Encrypting data is an essential component of any security strategy, as it protects organizations from various threats, such as data intrusions, ransomware attacks, and insider threats. Google Workspace enables organizations to manage who has access to their data and how it is utilized. This includes role-based access control (RBAC) and two-factor authentication (2FA) features. RBAC enables organizations to designate various roles to users, with each role having a unique set of permissions. Two-factor authentication (2FA) increases the security of user accounts by necessitating users to input a code that Google has sent to their mobile device in addition to their password when logging in. Google Workspace provides the capacity to audit security events for organizations. This allows organizations to determine who accessed their data, when, and what they did with it. Security auditing can help organizations identify and investigate suspicious activity, and it can also be used to comply with certain industry regulations and standards. Google Workspace offers numerous compliance tools to businesses, including data loss prevention (DLP) and data governance. DLP aids organizations in preventing the leak or accidental disclosure of sensitive data. Data governance enables organizations to administer their data consistently and compliantly. In addition to the features and services, Google Workspace Security and compliance includes several additional security features, such as:

- Detection and prevention of threats: Google Workspace employs numerous machine learning and artificial intelligence technologies to detect and prevent security threats.
- Google Workspace includes a team of security specialists who are available to assist organizations in responding to security incidents.
- Google Workspace offers security training to assist organizations in educating their personnel on security best practices.

Google Workspace Security and Compliance is a solution that can assist different organizations of all sizes in protecting their data and ensuring compliance with industry regulations and best practices. By utilizing Google Workspace Security and compliance, businesses can lessen or eliminate the risk of data breaches and other security incidents and ensure they are fulfilling their compliance obligations.

The following are examples of how Google Workspace Security and compliance can be utilized to protect data and assure compliance:

- A healthcare organization can use Google Workspace DLP to prevent breach or accidental disclosure of sensitive patient data.
- Using Google Workspace data governance, a financial services company can administer its financial data consistently and competently.
- Google Workspace security auditing enables a government agency to conform with regulations requiring them to monitor who accessed their data and what they did with it.
- A technology company can use Google Workspace threat detection and prevention to defend its data from malware and other security threats.
- An institution can utilize Google Workspace security training to educate its students and staff on security best practices.

Google Workspace Security and Compliance is a useful resource for businesses of all sizes. Organizations can protect their data, reduce the risk of security incidents, and ensure compliance with industry regulations and standards by utilizing Google Workspace Security and compliance.

9.1   Google Authenticator

Google Authenticator is an MFA program that users can make use of to add another layer of security to protect their Google Workspace account. MFA is a security measure that necessitates the use of two or more factors for identity verification. This is used to prevent unauthorized access to your account, even if an assailant knows your password.

Inner Functions of Google Authenticator

Google Authenticator generates unique credentials using a time-based one-time password (TOTP) algorithm. TOTP algorithms are time-based, so passwords change every 30 seconds. This makes it extremely challenging for adversaries to crack or acquire TOTP passwords.

Advantages of employing Google Authenticator:

- Using Google Authenticator to protect your Google Workspace account has several advantages, including the following:
- Google Authenticator adds another layer of security to your account, making it harder to access by unauthorized personnel.
- Google Authenticator can help lessen or eliminate the risk of deception, including phishing attacks and account takeovers.
- Numerous organizations mandate that employees utilize MFA to access company systems. Google Authenticator is a straightforward and efficient method for meeting these requirements.

How to get Google Authenticator

Follow the steps to set up Google Authenticator for your Google Workspace account:

- Search for "Google Authenticator Extension" using the Google search engine.

- Now click on the "Add" button to get the extension. I used Google Chrome in this example, but this extension should also work for other browsers.

- If done correctly, Google Authenticator will be added to the extensions section on the top right.

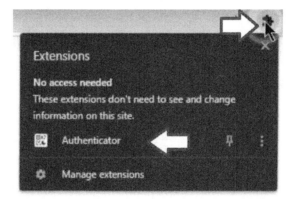

- Make sure to have the Google Authenticator pinned by clicking the pin icon

- Now, anytime you log into your accounts, you must manually enter a code or scan a QR code.

Using Google Authenticator: Hints

Here are some guidelines for effectively using Google Authenticator:

- Protect your alternative codes: The initial setup of Google Authenticator will generate a set of backup credentials. Ensure that you keep these codes in a secure location if you lose your phone or forget your PIN.
- Utilize a robust PIN: Your Google Authenticator PIN should be robust and distinct. Avoid using PINs that are easily guessed, like your birthday or anniversary.
- Google Authenticator can generate one-time passwords (OTPs) even when your phone is inactive. Ensure offline access is enabled in the app's settings.
- Google Authenticator is updated frequently with new security features. Ensure that you refresh the app whenever new updates become available.

Google Authenticator is a straightforward and efficient method for enabling MFA on your Google Workspace account. You can safeguard your account from unauthorized access and reduce the risk of fraudulent activities by using Google Authenticator.

9.2 User Roles and Permissions

User roles and permissions in Google Workspace allow organizations to control who has access to their data and what they can do with it. This is essential for security and compliance reasons. There are multiple Google Workspace user profiles, each with its own set of privileges. These are some of the most prevalent user roles:

- Super administrator: Super administrators have the most privileges and can administer all aspects of a Google Workspace account. This includes adding and removing users, assigning roles and permissions, and configuring security settings.
- Group administrators can manage user groups and their permissions. This includes adding and removing users from groups, allocating permissions and roles to groups, and configuring group settings.
- Users have the least privileges and can only access the data and applications to which they have been granted access. This includes their individual Gmail, Google Drive, and other Google Workspace applications.

In addition to these predefined roles, organizations can also create roles with unique permissions. This enables businesses to tailor user roles to their specific requirements. An organization could, for instance, establish a customized role for sales representatives that grants them access to customer contact information and sales data. The roles and permissions of Google Workspace users are defined using a role-based access control (RBAC) model. RBAC is a security model that allocates users permissions based on their organizational role. This makes it simple to manage user permissions and ensure that users have only the permissions necessary to perform their tasks.

User roles and permissions in Google Workspace can be used to control access to a variety of data and applications, including:

- Google mail
- Google Docs
- Calendar from Google
- Google Docs, Google Sheets, and Google PowerPoint slides.
- Google Chat and Google Meet
- GCP (Google Cloud Platform)
- Google Workspace Applications Market

By utilizing user roles and permissions in Google Workspace, organizations can defend their data, ensure compliance, and increase productivity. Here are some suggestions for effectively administering Google Workspace user roles and permissions:

- Clearly define user roles and permissions: Before designating user roles and permissions, take the time to define the capabilities of each role. This will ensure that users have only the permissions required to perform their tasks.
- Utilize groups to manage permissions for users: By using groups, it is possible to administer the permissions of multiple users simultaneously. This simplifies the management of user permissions and makes it simpler to ensure that each user properly possesses the necessary information.
- Utilize custom rules to establish granular permissions: Custom rules can be used to grant permissions to users or user groups. This can be helpful for organizations that need to modify user roles to their requirements.

- Regularly review user roles and permissions: User duties and permissions should be reviewed frequently to ensure their continued relevance. For instance, if an employee departs the company, their user role and permissions should be removed.

By adhering to these recommendations, organizations can use Google Workspace user roles and permissions to safeguard their data, ensure compliance, and boost productivity.

9.3 Two-Factor Authentication

A security feature known as Two-factor authentication (2FA) adds another layer of protection to your Google Workspace account. When 2FA is enabled, you will be required to input a one-time password (OTP) in addition to your Google Workspace password when logging in. This OTP can be generated using a variety of methods, such as a text message, a phone call, or a mobile authentication app.

How Google Workspace 2FA functions

When 2FA is enabled, you will be required to input your password when logging into your Google Workspace account. After entering your password, you will be asked to input an OTP. The OTP can be generated using a variety of methods, such as a text message, a phone call, or a mobile authentication app. Using a mobile authentication program, such as Google Authenticator, generates a new OTP every 30 second. The OTP is based on a time-based one-time password (TOTP) algorithm, making it extremely challenging for attackers to predict or steal. After generating an OTP, enter it on the Google Workspace login page and select Sign in. You will be entered into your Google Workspace account if the OTP is valid.

Advantages of employing Google Workspace 2FA

There are numerous advantages to utilizing Google Workspace 2FA, including:

- Increased security: Two-factor authentication (2FA) adds an additional layer of security to your account, making it very difficult for unauthorized users to gain access. Even if an adversary knows your password, they cannot access your account without the OTP.

- Reduced risk of fraud Two-factor authentication can help reduce the risk of fraud, including phishing attacks and account takeovers. Account takeovers occur when an attacker obtains control of a user's account, whereas phishing attacks attempt to trick users into divulging their passwords. By requiring users to input an OTP and their password, 2FA can help protect against these attacks.

- Observance: Numerous organizations require employees to use two-factor authentication to access company systems. Two-factor authentication is a simple and effective method to meet these requirements.

Configuring Google Workspace 2FA

Follow these steps to set up Google Workspace 2FA for your account:

- Go to Google's administrative console.
- On the left side, you can find the "Security" icon and click it.

- On the Security tab, look for "Configure 2-Step Verification policies" and click on that.

2-Step Verification

Configure 2-Step Verification policies

- Choose the authentication method you wish to employ.
- Follow the provided instructions to finalize the two-step verification.

After enabling 2FA for your Google Workspace account, you will be prompted to input an OTP whenever you attempt to log in. Ensure that your OTP-generating device is secure and easily accessible.

Tips for effectively using Google Workspace 2FA

Here are some guidelines for effectively using Google Workspace 2FA:

- Employ a robust authentication method: Choose a strong authentication method, such as a mobile authentication program, when configuring 2FA. Text messages and phone calls are insecure authentication methods because an adversary can intercept them.
- Safeguard your OTP-generating device: a safe device is a secure device. This implies that you should store it in a secure manner and not share it with anyone else.
- Have a secondary strategy: Be sure to have a fallback plan if you lose your OTP-generating device or are unable to access it. This may entail the use of a backup code or the configuration of a trusted device.

Google Workspace 2FA is valuable for preventing unauthorized access to your account. By enabling 2FA, you can enhance account security and reduce the risk of fraud.

9.4 Compliance and Certification

Compliance and certification for Google Workspace refers to Google's commitment to meeting the security, privacy, and compliance needs of its consumers. Google Workspace is certified in accordance with a vast array of industry standards and regulations, including:

- Information Security Management ISO/IEC 27001
- ISO/IEC 27017 (Cloud Security) is a standard for cloud security.
- ISO/IEC 27018 (Cloud Privacy) is a standard for cloud privacy.
- ISO/IEC 27701 (Privacy) is a privacy standard.
- The HIPAA GDPR
- The PCI DSS

In addition to complying with the CCPA, SOC 2, and FedRAMP, Google Workspace adheres to several other industry standards and regulations.

How Google Workspace certification and compliance functions

Compliance and certification for Google Workspace are attained through a combination of organizational and technical measures. Encryption, access controls, and security audits are examples of technical standards. Security policies and procedures, employee training, and routine security audits are among the organizational measures. Google is also subject to regular audits by third-party auditors to ensure that it complies with the certified industry standards and regulations.

Google Workspace compliance and certification advantages

Using Google Workspace compliance and certification has several advantages, including:

- Risk of data vulnerabilities and security incidents is diminished: Compliance and certification for Google Workspace reduce or eliminate the risk of data breach and security incidents by requiring Google to adhere to numerous industry standards and regulations.
- Increased adherence to industry standards and rules: Compliance and certification for Google Workspace enables organizations to conform to industry standards and regulations, such as HIPAA and GDPR.
- Increased customer trust: Google Workspace compliance and certification facilitate the development of customer trust by demonstrating an organization's dedication to safeguarding customer data and adhering to applicable industry standards and regulations.

How to use Google Workspace certification and compliance

To use Google Workspace compliance and certification, organizations must first identify the applicable industry standards and regulations. Once they have identified the applicable standards and regulations, they can review Google Workspace's compliance documentation to determine how Google Workspace satisfies their requirements. Contacting Google Workspace support for assistance with compliance and certification is also an option for organizations. Compliance and certification for Google Workspace is a valuable resource for businesses of all sizes. By utilizing Google Workspace, businesses can reduce the risk of data breaches and security incidents, improve their compliance with industry standards and regulations, and boost consumer confidence.

9.5 Auditing and Monitoring

Auditing and monitoring Google Workspace is the process of observing and analyzing user activity in Google Workspace applications. This can be accomplished by identifying and investigating security incidents, enhancing compliance, and maximizing user productivity.

How Google Workspace monitoring and auditing functions

Google Workspace offers audit records and monitoring reports that can be used to monitor and analyze user activity. Audit logs contain comprehensive information about user activity, such as the user who performed the action, the action that was performed, and the date and time the action was performed. Monitoring reports summarize user activity, such as the number of users who logged in to a specific application on a given day or the amount of time spent by users on specific duties.

Auditing and monitoring of Google Workspace can be used for a variety of purposes, including:

- Auditing and monitoring of Google Workspace can be used to identify and investigate security incidents, such as unauthorized account access and data breaches. For example, administrators can use audit logs to identify users who have logged in from peculiar locations or who have accessed sensitive files.

- Google Workspace auditing and monitoring can be useful in demonstrating compliance with industry regulations and standards, such as HIPAA and GDPR. For instance, administrators can use audit logs to demonstrate that users do not access or share sensitive information with unauthorized parties.

- Auditing and monitoring of Google Workspace can be used to identify areas where user productivity can be enhanced. For instance, administrators can use audit records to identify users who spend excessive time on non-work-related activities or who struggle to complete tasks.

How to effectively use Google Workspace auditing and monitoring

Here are some strategies for effectively utilizing Google Workspace auditing and monitoring:

- Identify your objectives: What are your Google Workspace auditing and monitoring goals? Do you wish to enhance security, compliance, or efficiency? Know your objectives, and then you can begin identifying the audit records, monitoring reports, and alerts you require.

- Configure settings for auditing and monitoring: Google Workspace offers numerous auditing and monitoring options. You can tailor these parameters to your specific requirements. For instance, audit logs can be configured to record all user activity or only specific classes of user activity. You can also configure daily, weekly, or monthly monitoring report generation.

- Regularly review audit records and monitoring reports: Reviewing audit logs and monitoring reports on a regular basis will help identify security incidents, compliance issues, and areas where user productivity can be enhanced. For instance, administrators can examine audit records to identify users who have accessed sensitive files or logged in from unusual locations. Administrators can also examine monitoring reports to identify users who spend significant time on non-work-related activities or struggle to complete tasks.

- Configure alerts Administrators can configure alerts to be notified of specific events, such as when a user signs in from an unusual location or when a sensitive file is accessed. This can aid administrators in rapidly identifying and responding to security incidents.

Auditing and monitoring of Google Workspace is a valuable resource for businesses of all sizes. Organizations can use Google Workspace auditing and monitoring to increase their security, compliance, and productivity.

Uses of Google Workspace auditing and monitoring include the following:

- An administrator can use audit records to identify users who have accessed sensitive files or logged in from unusual locations. The administrator can then contact these users to investigate suspicious behavior.
- Compliance: An administrator can use monitoring reports to demonstrate that users do not access or share sensitive information with unauthorized parties. This can help the company adhere to industry standards and regulations.
- An administrator can identify users who spend excessive time on non-work-related activities by analyzing audit records. The administrator can then discuss ways for these users to increase their productivity.

Google Workspace auditing and monitoring is a potent instrument that organizations of all sizes can use to enhance their security, compliance, and productivity.

10 TIPS, TRICKS & TROUBLESHOOTING

10.1 Lesser-known Features

Smart Compose:
Smart Compose in Google Docs: Smart Compose is a feature that enables you to compose emails and documents more quickly and accurately by suggesting the next word or phrase you intend to type. It can also assist with correcting grammar and punctuation mistakes. Smart Compose learns your writing style and preferences through machine learning. Over time, it will become more adept at suggesting pertinent words and phrases as you write. To enable Smart, Compose, check the box next to Enable Smart Compose in the Tools > Preferences > Smart Compose menu.

Explore:
Explore in Google Sheets: Explore is a tool for analyzing your data and discovering trends and patterns. Explore can be used to generate charts and diagrams and conduct statistical analysis.
Select the data you wish to analyze and click the Explore icon to use Explore. Explore will then open a new window in which you can construct graphs and charts and conduct statistical analysis.

Connected Sheets:
Connected Sheets enables merging data from multiple spreadsheets into a single spreadsheet. This can be beneficial for data analysis and report creation.
To connect two spreadsheets, open the spreadsheet you wish to link to the other and select the Data menu. After selecting Connected Sheets, click the Add icon.

Google Assistant:
Google Assistant can be the assistant you need to help you control the different Google Workspace applications, including Gmail, Calendar, and Docs. You can use Google Assistant to schedule a meeting in Calendar or create a new document in Docs, for instance.
Say "Hi, Google" or "Hello, Google," and then deliver your command to activate Google Assistant. Example: "Hi, Google, schedule a meeting with Jane Doe tomorrow at 8 a.m."

Google Sites:
Google Sites is a website builder that enables the creation of basic websites without the need for coding knowledge. Google Sites is an easy and efficient website creation application that can be used for

businesses, personal endeavors, and education. To create a new website, go to Google Sites and select the plus sign (+). Then, you can select a site template and begin adding content.

Google Cloud Search:

Google Cloud Search is a search engine that can search across all your Google Workspace applications and other Google Cloud Platform services. This is a great approach to locate the information quickly and easily you require. To use Google Cloud Search, navigate to Google Cloud Search and enter your query. Then, Google Cloud Search will yield results from all your Google Workspace applications and other Google Cloud Platform services.

10.2 Troubleshooting Common Issues

Google Workspace troubleshooting can be performed in a variety of methods, depending on the nature of the problem being encountered. Here are some guidelines:

- Reboot the device. This can frequently resolve minor software issues.
- Verify the Internet connection. Ensure you have a solid and consistent internet connection.
- Remove all browser cache and cookies. This can eliminate any potentially problematic data corruption.
- Try an alternative web browser. If you are experiencing compatibility issues with one browser, try another to see if the issue persists.
- The browser and operating system should be updated. Ensure you are using the most recent browser and operating system versions.
- Contact support for Google Workspace. If issues persist even after trying different solutions, you can contact Google Workspace support for further assistance.

Here are some specific troubleshooting guidelines for frequent Google Workspace issues:

If you are experiencing issues with Google Workspace, consider the following:

- Verify that the password you entered is accurate.
- Try erasing or clearing the cache and cookies from your browser.
- Try an alternative web browser.
- Ensure that you are submitting the correct code when utilizing two-factor authentication (2FA).
- Contact Google Workspace support if you're still having difficulty signing in.

If you are experiencing issues with Gmail, consider the following:

- Examine the spam folder. Erroneous email filtering is causing your spam folder to be populated with unwanted messages.
- Ensure that you have sufficient space in your Gmail account. If storage space is exhausted, deleting old emails or purchasing more may be necessary.
- Try an alternative web browser. If you are experiencing issues with Gmail in one browser, attempt a different browser to determine if the issue persists.

If you are experiencing issues with Google Drive, consider the following:

- Verify the Internet connection. Ensure you have a solid and consistent internet connection.
- Try again to upload or download your assets. A network problem may have interrupted the file transfer.
- Try another web browser. If you are experiencing issues with Google Drive in one browser, attempt a different browser to determine if the issue persists.

If you are experiencing issues with Google Docs, Sheets, and Slides, attempt the following:

- Ensure you have access to the Internet. Google Docs, Sheets, and Slides cannot function without an internet connection.
- Try refreshing the web page. If the page fails to load correctly, reload it.

- Try an alternative web browser. If you are experiencing issues with Google Docs, Sheets, or Slides in one browser, try another one to see if the issue persists.
- Again, if the issue persists, Google Workspace support can be contacted for further assistance.

Here are some additional troubleshooting tips for Google Workspace:

- Describe the issue as precisely as feasible to Google Workspace support. Provide simple and specific details of your problem to make it easier for Google Workspace support to help you resolve the issue.
- Provide as much detail about your device and software environment as feasible. This information can assist Google Workspace support in identifying the source of the issue.
- Have patience. It may take some time for Google Workspace support to resolve the issue.

10.3 FAQ: Frequently Asked Questions

What does Google Workspace entail?

- Google Workspace is a cloud-based application focused on a collaboration and productivity platform for enterprises and organizations. It includes Gmail, Calendar, Drive, Docs, Sheets, Slides, and Meet, among other applications.

What advantages does using Google Workspace offer?

- Google Workspace features are designed to increase your efficiency and effectiveness at work. For instance, Google Docs, Sheets, and Slides make it simple to create and collaborate on documents, spreadsheets, and presentations. Gmail also facilitates more efficient email management.
- Google Workspace's collaborative tools facilitate working with others on projects and duties. For instance, you can share documents, spreadsheets, and presentations with others and collaborate in real-time on documents.
- Google Workspace is a subscription-based service, so you do not need to purchase or maintain software. Moreover, Google Workspace can help you save money by removing the need for paper and other physical resources.
- Google Workspace provides numerous security features to safeguard your data. Google Workspace offers several security features to help you detect and prevent malware and phishing attacks, such as encrypting all data at rest and in transit and encrypting all data in transit.

What is the cost of Google Workspace?

- Google Workspace provides a range of pricing options to accommodate enterprises and organizations of all sizes. You can begin with a free plan that includes Gmail, Google Calendar, and Google Drive. You can upgrade to a paid plan for additional storage capacity and features.

How do I begin using Google Workspace?

- Create a Google Workspace account to get started with Google Workspace. After account creation is done, you can then begin using Google Workspace tools to manage your email, calendar, and documents, among other things.

How can I obtain additional information about Google Workspace?

- There are numerous resources available to assist you in learning more about Google Workspace. Visit the Google Workspace website or enroll in a Google Workspace training course.

Are custom domains allowed in Google Workspace?

- Yes, your own domain name can be used with Google Workspace. This will give your company or organization an air of professionalism.

Can Google Workspace be used offline?

- Yes, Google Workspace can be used offline. You can download the Google Workspace app for your mobile devices, which allows you to work offline on Google Workspace documents.

Google Workspace: Is it secure?

- Google Workspace is secure, yes. Google Workspace protects your data with a variety of security features, including encryption, access controls, and security auditing.

Can I receive assistance with Google Workspace?

- Yes, support for Google Workspace is available. Support options for Google Workspace include email, phone, and live chat.

11   ADDITIONAL RESOURCES

11.1 Glossary

Arrays - In Google Sheets, arrays are data collections comprised of rows and columns.

Cloud-based platform - Anything that entails the delivery of hosted services over the internet, and users can gain access, share, store, and secure information in a remote server called a "cloud."

CSV (Comma-separated Values) - A text file with a particular format that enables data to be stored in a table-structured format.

Database - It is an organized collection of structured information or data, which is usually stored electronically on a computer system.

Email - A system for electronically transmitting written communications from one computer to another. Examples are Gmail, Yahoo mail, etc.

Formula - This is used for performing mathematical calculations.

Function – In Google Sheets, a predefined formula calculates specified values in a specific order.

Gigabyte (GB) - It is a unit of data storage capacity equal to approximately 1 billion bytes.

HTML - The Hypertext Markup Language standardizes the labeling of text files to accomplish font, color, graphic, and link effects on World Wide Web pages.

Integer - Is a non-fractional whole number that can be positive, negative, or zero.

Internet - A global network of electronic communications that links computer networks and organizational computer facilities.

PDF (Portable Document Format) - A document format that provides an electronic image of printed text or text and illustrations that can be viewed, printed, and electronically transmitted.

PST (personal storage table) - Microsoft's file format for storing objects such as calendar events, contacts, and email messages.

Real-time - Actual length of time for a given process or event.

Search Engine – A software application that people use for searching for information online using keywords or phrases. Examples are Google, Yahoo, Bing, etc.

String - The text from which you wish to extract data

Social Networking – Utilizes social media platforms to connect with new and existing acquaintances, family members, coworkers, and businesses.

Software Applications - It is a type of software that allows users to perform specific tasks by interacting with them directly.

Subscription - Making or agreeing to make a payment in advance to receive or partake in something.

URL (Uniform Resource Locator) - This is the location of a website.

Version History - It provides you with a running list of the changes in your files over their lifetimes.

Web Browser - A program used to access information from the World Wide Web. Examples are Google Chrome, Firefox, Brave, etc.

XML (Extensible Markup Language) - Transmits metadata that specifies the structure of any tabular dataset.

ZIP - An archive file format can contain multiple files combined and compressed into a single file.

11.2 Google Workspace Updates and News

Latest Google Workspace updates and news in 2023:

- Google Meet's new conference features are Google Meet has been updated with several new features, such as a new user interface, noise suppression, and closed captions.
- Improved collaboration features in Google Docs, Sheets, and Slides: Google Docs, Sheets, and Slides have been updated with several new collaboration features, including the ability to add comments and suggestions to the work of others and to monitor changes in real time.
- Google Workspace has been updated with several new security features, including the ability to set up two-factor authentication for all users and audit user activity.
- Google Workspace has been updated with several new pricing plans to accommodate enterprises and organizations of all sizes.
- New integrations with other tools and services: Google Workspace has been updated with several new integrations with other tools and services, including Zoom, Slack, and Asana.

In addition to these enhancements, Google Workspace will soon receive several new features and products, as announced by Google. Included are:

- Google Smart Canvas is a new set of features that will simplify collaborating with others on projects and duties. Smart Canvas includes the ability to insert smart chips into documents as well as the capacity to construct interactive whiteboards.
- Google Meet will shortly enable the recording of meeting transcripts. This will simplify examining meeting notes and sharing them with others.
- Google Workspace Essentials: Google Workspace Essentials is a new subscription plan geared toward small enterprises and organizations. Workspace Essentials comprises the most popular Google Workspace applications, from Gmail, Docs, Drive, Calendar, Slides, and Sheets.

New features and products are continuously introduced to Google Workspace, which continually evolves. By keeping abreast of the most recent Google Workspace news and updates, you can maximize your Google Workspace subscription.

11.3 Recommended Third-Party Tools

Recommended third-party applications for Google Workspace:

- Zoom is an application used for videoconferencing which can be utilized for meetings, webinars, and training sessions. Zoom provides many features, including screen sharing, breakout rooms, and recording.
- Slack is an application used for team communication that can be used for sharing files, messaging, and video conferencing. Slack also integrates with a variety of other applications, including Google Workspace and Zoom.
- Asana is a project management application that can be utilized to monitor assignments, deadlines, and progress. Asana also offers integrations with other applications, including Google Workspace and Slack.
- Trello is a project management application that visualizes work using Kanban boards. Trello can be utilized for a variety of initiatives, including software development, marketing, and customer support.
- Canva is a web application for creating social media graphics, presentations, and other visual content. Canva is simple to use and provides a selection of templates and stock images to help you get started.
- Grammarly is a grammar and spelling checker used to enhance writing. Grammarly offers numerous features, including plagiarism detection and style recommendations.

These are only a few third-party utilities compatible with Google Workspace. When selecting a third-party application, it is essential to consider your requirements and budgets. Additionally, check if the application is compatible with Google Workspace.

Here are some additional guidelines for selecting and utilizing third-party applications with Google Workspace:

- Ensure the tool's safety. When selecting a third-party application, it is essential to ensure its security. Check the security features and read the privacy statement of the tool.
- Ensure that the tool is Google Workspace compatible. When selecting a third-party application, ensuring compatibility with Google Workspace is essential. Check the website of the instrument for compatibility information.
- Check the evaluations of the tool. Before selecting a third-party tool, it is advisable to peruse user evaluations. This can aid in identifying any prospective issues with the tool.
- Start with a trial period. Numerous third-party resources provide complimentary trials. This is an excellent method to test out a tool before purchasing it.

By following these guidelines, you'll be able to select and utilize third-party tools to improve your Google Workspace experience.

12 CONCLUSION

Since its 1998 inception, Google has expanded from a search engine to offering diverse services, impacting daily life and work significantly. Gmail, Google Drive, and Google Meet simplify communication, file-sharing, and virtual interaction for billions worldwide. Recognized as a leading tech firm, Google continuously evolves and innovates its products, delving into AI, machine learning, and augmented reality. Products like Google Search and Gmail have become smarter and more secure, with Google Drive integrating better with Google Workspace. Google Workspace stands as a crucial tool for businesses enhancing productivity and collaboration, offering scalable and continually updated solutions. It's seamlessly integrated into daily life, accessible with a click or tap, removing traditional tool constraints. As Google persists in its technological advancement, it's vital to stay updated and utilize its ever-evolving tools, ubiquitous in homes, workplaces, schools, and society at large.

13 BONUS

Simply scan the QR code below to navigate to a special page. By entering your email there, you'll unlock access to exclusive bonuses such as video explanations, courses, and mobile apps. Your participation and feedback are highly valued—thank you for engaging!

LINK: https://BookHip.com/RJRTVVB

Printed in Great Britain
by Amazon

36753942R00066